GOD'S CREATURES
in GOD'S WORD

Editors: Warren and Paula Berkley

ONESTONE
BIBLICAL RESOURCES

Published by:
One Stone Press
979 Lovers Lane
Bowling Green, KY 42103

Printed in the United States of America

ISBN 13: 978-1-941422-53-3

www.onestone.com

Contents

Note: Websites referenced in this book were verified at time of publication, but may have changed ownership or content after release of the book.

Dedication

John Allen

Foreword

My wife and I have enjoyed having a part in publishing several books over the past decade. That interest has caused us to explore various title and content ideas together. Often, when we travel together, we brainstorm book ideas. While many of those ideas never reach the ink-on-paper destination, a few make the cut.

Several years ago we entertained the idea of a book about the animal imagery of the Bible. Scripture is rich with imagery, symbols and illustrations designed for the benefit of the reader. Agricultural illustrations form the basis of several parables. Within that genre there are animals, which were familiar to the original readers or hearers of God's message.

What do we know of those creatures? And if we are not familiar with them, does that put us at some disadvantage in reading the writer's use of those animals?

We've put this book together to help modern readers better understand the animal imagery in the Bible. (And there may be a volume two in the future.)

As this idea developed in our conversations, we thought it best to use writers with direct experience with these animals and corresponding academic background. Veterinarians, experts in zoology, a marine biologist and other highly qualified Christians who are good Bible students have contributed to the content of this book.

Our hope is this book will help Bible students. Likewise it will become a good reference book and for many, an intriguing book for a good read. It should help guide us into those passages where God's creatures are referenced in God's Word. Let these animals "speak" to you and help you dig deeper into Scripture.

Acknowledgements and gratitude are in order to each of our writers. These are men with full-time professional commitments, who agreed to sign on to an additional project, being committed to helping Bible students in this subject area. Their proof-readers are to be recognized along with those who assisted them in research. We are thankful to our consulting editor and cover designer, Marc Hinds. Andy Alexander and his team at One Stone have applied their skill to the project. Ron Kirkwood deserves recognition for the photo contribution. Above all we are thankful to God, who is seeking through His Word to reach us, help us and save us. To Jesus, we give our praise for His supreme love and care. And may great blessings continue through Sacred Selections, the worthy recipient of the proceeds from this book.

—Warren and Paula Berkley
January 2020

The Eagle

by Bill Baker

"You have seen what I did to the Egyptians, and how I bore
you on eagles' wings and brought you to Myself."
(Exodus 19:4)

In the first chapter of Genesis Moses records that on the fifth day God created winged fowl to fly above the earth in the open firmament of heaven. The fact that birds were created on the fifth day may not grab the attention of many readers, and to many it is probably viewed as just another group of animals created in the first week of creation. However, birds are important and are referenced throughout the Bible from Genesis to the Revelation. The diversity of birds and their abilities to fly, to communicate, to hunt, to migrate, and to reproduce reflects the amazing design of the Creator. Today, birds can still be found over all lands and seas. Some are resident and travel very little, while others travel thousands of miles during their lifetime as they seasonally migrate. While there are many amazing species that catch the attention of us all, the eagles from the family *Accipitridae*, possess traits that separate them from all others.

While we typically consider the lion the king of terrestrial beasts, the eagle, throughout time, has been the unquestioned master and ruler of the skies. Throughout history this impressive wonder of the avian world has been revered for its amazing speed, tremendous power, keen vision, and aerial stamina. Its figure has been chiseled from stone and from wood for millennia. Its form has been found etched on walls of caves, on the tombs of the ancients, and its name even recorded on papyrus. Today the eagle resides in the coat of arms of at least 25 different countries. In the mind of man, the eagle has forever stood out from other species that occupy the skies above.

There are approximately 59 species of eagles scattered throughout the earth's continents, with only two found in North America. The great majority, 46 species, are found in Eurasia and Africa. While there are physical differences among these species, they possess a host of analogous traits that set them apart from other birds of prey.

Eagles are typically characterized by their long and wide wings, heavy heads, strong hooked bills that are heavier than bills of other raptors, powerful legs, sharp talons, and vision that is five times better than that of humans. Their bodies are covered with approximately 7,000 feathers that provide it with the ability to stay aloft for extended periods of time, soaring effortlessly among the sky's thermals.

Eagles are very large, with wingspans of many species extending 7-8 feet. Their size, powerful muscles, and long and broad wings combine to give them the ability to dive at prodigious speed and capture prey virtually undetected. The Golden Eagle, found in the western U.S., is the fastest of the species being clocked at almost 200 mph in a stoop.[1]

We marvel at the ability of the eagle to command the skies. It is said among ornithologists that the eagle is the only bird of prey that does not quickly glance over its shoulder just before attacking its prey. The eagle has no fear of other predators coming in behind it to share its prey.[2] They truly are the masters and rulers of the sky.

One of the most prominent examples of ancient texts recording various traits of the eagle is the Bible. The eagle is mentioned approximately 40 times in the Old and New Testaments in a variety of contexts. The majority use the eagle in a figurative sense, comparing some element of the eagle's physical capabilities or structure to describe events, visions, and sometimes people. In most cases the description is of a common trait the eagle possesses that when read, can be easily understood. In some cases, a more in-depth understanding of the biological traits of the eagle will help us come to a better understanding of the scriptural texts.

The intent of this chapter is to strengthen the reader's knowledge of a group of biological peculiarities the eagles possess, which should subsequently lead to a better understanding of what the inspired writers had to say.

In Exodus 19:4, Moses records this grand message from Jehovah: "Ye have seen what I did unto the Egyptians, and how I bare you on eagles' wings, and brought you unto myself." In this context we see where God declares that he brought the Hebrew people out of the land of Egypt unto himself. Recall the great power and might God revealed to his people and the Egyptians through a series of plagues that wreaked havoc on the Egyptian way of life and belittled their idols of stone and wood. Gods supremacy was no match for the idolatrous gods of the Egyptians.

God's parting of the Red Sea was the culminating act in delivering the Israelites to safety and simultaneously providing the final blow to the Egyptian army. Unparalleled power is figuratively described in the eagles' wings delivering God's people to safety. God has delivered them out from under the threat of their enemy by the awesome display of power wrought in the wings of the eagle.

Having a better understanding of the eagle's wing structure and flight capabilities gives us a better appreciation of the imagery God provides in this passage. In general, large species of eagles, such as the American Bald Eagle, have skeletons that weigh only about 0.5 pounds (250-300 grams). Their bones are relatively thin and hollow throughout, hence the incredibly low skeletal weight. Providing the power for wing movement are a pair of muscles running from the keel of the breastbone to the humerus bone, the pectoralis and the supracoracoideus. These muscles are in the breast of the eagle, a unique arrangement in birds of flight as they are below the wings and operate like a rope and pulley system to provide a low center of gravity which leads to the bird's aerodynamic stability. These two muscles are antagonistic (one muscle opposing another muscle), the supracoracoideus providing the upstroke and the pectoralis providing the downstroke. Their broad wings are covered with overlapping layers of feathers that are controlled to provide optimal air flow for both power and speed. Relative to their size, eagles' wings contain more power and strength than the wings of an airplane.

The prophet Isaiah employs the wings of the eagle to provide a comforting and powerful message to those in captivity who put their faith and hope in Jehovah. In Isaiah 40:29-31 the inspired prophet provides us with the following assurance: "He giveth power to the faint; and to them that have no might he increaseth strength. Even the youths shall faint and be weary, and the young men shall utterly fall: But they that wait upon the Lord shall renew their strength; they shall mount up with wings as eagles; they shall run, and not be weary; and they shall walk, and faint not." With God's people in Babylonian captivity, Isaiah presents a contrast between the failures of the strength of the young and the renewed strength of those that rely on Jehovah for their sustaining power. The strength provided for those who rely on Jehovah is described in this text as "mounting up with the wings of eagles." Figuratively speaking these are the same eagles' wings Jehovah provided to the children of Israel when they were removed from Egyptian bondage. They are powerful, they are swift, they are sustaining, and they are available for all who lean on Jehovah for their strength.

A similar example of the formidable strength of the eagle's wings can be found in Revelation 12:14, where John records the following: "And to the woman were given two wings of a great eagle, that she might fly into the wilderness, into her place." The figurative language used here in the apocalypse paints a picture of a woman being given mighty eagle's wings to escape the persecution of the cruel Roman Empire and find refuge. This woman represents those followers of God that are suffering persecution at the hands of men, in this case the cruel emperors of the Roman Empire. Here again we find God providing a refuge and strength for his obedient follower in the form of the mighty eagle's wings. As noted in Exodus 19:4 and Isaiah 40:31, these wings are the ultimate descriptor of the relief God provides for his obedient people.

A compliment to the incredible power of the eagle's wings is speed. Eagles wings, along with specialized musculature, a light skeleton, and an abundance of specialized feathers, provide the ability to propel this dynamic bird at great speeds. An array of impressive statistics catches one's attention regarding the flight speed of an eagle. The golden eagle, native to the western United States, has an average flight speed during casual soaring of 28-32 mph, but while hunting or displaying it can attain gliding speeds of up to 120 mph. When diving (also known as stooping) for prey, or during territorial displays, the golden eagle can reach maximum speeds of 150-200 mph. I have witnessed an adult golden eagle capture a rabbit running at top speed across the Mojave Desert. The eagle, from an altitude of approximately 1,500 ft, entered his stoop and swiftly descended, sweeping the rabbit off the desert floor in the blink of an eye. What appeared to be a fleet-footed creature leaving a slight trail of dust as it scampered through creosote and yucca plants, was overwhelmed by the incredible speed and power of the attacking golden eagle. The swiftness and accuracy of this magnificent predator coming from high above is nothing short of amazing.

In Deuteronomy 28:49 Moses referenced the speed of the eagle when he was warning the Israelites of the consequences of future disobedience. The inspired text reveals the following: "The Lord will bring a nation against you from afar, from the end of the earth, as swift as the eagle flies, a nation whose language you will not understand." Here we find a clear message to the Israelites regarding the consequences of disobedience. Destruction would come from afar without warning because of the speed with which the enemy approaches. The eagle, known for its amazing wing strength, is now described in this text as also being a very swift flier. The eagle, like the enemies of a disobedient people, is in fact rapid, is silent in its approach, and brings sudden destruction to its prey.

An amazing trait that allows the eagle to attack its prey from long distances is its remarkable vision. Several eagle species are able to see their prey thousands of feet away and can easily detect the movements of field mice while flying as high as 650 feet above the ground.[3] There are two features of an eagle's eyes that give it such sharp vision. First, its' retina has more light-detecting cells, or cones, than humans. This allows the eagle to detect very fine details. Second, the eagle has a much deeper fovea than we have. Fovea are the cone-rich structures in the backs of the eyes that detect light from the center of the visual field. This feature appears to allow the eyes to function like a telephoto lens.[4] It is believed that an eagle can spot an ant crawling on the ground from atop a 10-story building, or a rabbit from two miles away. As he drops from the sky to attack his prey, the muscles of his eyes make constant adjustments to the curvature of the eyeballs, enabling him to keep his prey in sharp focus as he makes his approach. While man views 20/20 vision as excellent, the eagles' vision is 20/5. Furthermore, our peripheral view is approximately 180 degrees while the eagle has a 340 degrees field of view.[5]

In making application to the text of Deuteronomy 28:49, we now understand how this swift flying predator can focus on its prey from great distances undetected, and swoop down upon its' prey without warning, delivering catastrophic destruction in the blink of an eye. The keen eyesight of the eagle provides guidance, helping the swift flying eagle succeed with its objective.

Later in the history of the Israelites we see the warning provided by Moses in Deuteronomy repeated by the prophet Hosea as the northern tribes are about to fall to the Assyrian Empire. In Hosea 8:1 the prophet writes, "Set the trumpet to thy mouth. He shall come as an eagle against the house of the Lord, because they have transgressed my covenant, and trespassed against my law." Hosea, prophet of Israel, is warning God's people of the swiftness with which they will be defeated because of their continued disobedience. The invading army will come swiftly and without warning and will show no mercy to its prey. Hosea's warning should have been a reminder to them of the words Moses spoke centuries before, as the swiftness of the eagle was known and understood by all. That warning is one of repentance from wickedness that separates them from the Lord, and a return to obedience where they will find the comfort and protection of the Lord. History tells us that there was no repentance and the fall of Israel to Assyria was rapid and complete.

To provide even more context to the statements of Moses and Hosea we can apply another remarkable fact associated with the eagle. As mentioned previously, most raptors, such as hawks and falcons, will take a quick glance over their shoulder just prior to attacking their prey. They are on the look-out for others that may prey on them or might have thoughts of taking their kill. Contrary to this behavior, the eagle, never looks back! He is the master and ruler of the skies and fears no other aerial predator. He intensely focuses on his prey, showing no signs of fear or trepidation, only the determined will to swiftly capture his prey. God, through his prophet Hosea, is telling the wicked in Israel that the conquering army will arrive without warning and will exhibit the speed, determination, and destructive power characteristic of the eagle. There would be no escape from the fate their disobedience brought upon them. They had failed to repent and turn to the Lord and must suffer the consequences.

The northern tribes were not alone in their wicked disobedience to God. Following the fall of Israel to the Assyrians we find Jeremiah encouraging the people of Judah to repent. The prophet makes the following statement in chapter 4, verse 13, "Behold, he shall come up like clouds, and his chariots like a whirlwind. His horses are swifter than eagles. Woe to us, for we are plundered!" Those living in Judah had knowledge of the Assyrian invasion of the northern tribes and knew of the prophecies made against them for their continued wickedness. Jeremiah describes similar destruction upon Judah if they failed to repent. The figurative language we find here is quite similar to the words of Hosea. In this instance we find Jeremiah describing to those of Judah that the invading army's horses would be swifter than eagles! We now have a clearer understanding of how fast that is, and we know many of the traits that factor into this speed. We also now have a better understanding of how the eagle focuses on its prey, fearing no others. Those in Judah knew exactly what Jeremiah was describing, but they too failed to repent and were overwhelmed by the invading Babylonian armies.

Too often pride stands in the way of man's obedience to God. We find an example of this in Jeremiah 49:16 where the prophet pronounces to the Ammonites, "Your fierceness has deceived you, the pride of your heart, O you who dwell in the clefts of the rock, who hold the height of the hill! Though you make your nests as high as the eagle, I will bring you down from there, says the Lord." In this context Jeremiah describes the self-securing pride the Ammonites displayed. Here, judgment is pronounced upon the Ammonites. They were a strong and terrible people, living among the high rocks of the hills. However, even if they made their fortresses as high as the eagles' nest, they would be brought down.

Most species of eagles are known to do this very thing. They construct nests in the clefts of high rocks or amongst strong branches of the highest trees. They do this for security, for prey opportunities, and to command the realm around the nest and to oversee the surrounding territory. Job makes reference to this in chapter 39, verses 27-29 where he states, "Doth the eagle mount up at thy command, and make her nest on high? She dwelleth and abideth on the rock, upon the crag of the rock, and the strong place. From thence she seeketh the prey, and her eyes behold afar off."

In North America the bald eagle is a great example of how we can apply the figurative language of this passage. The bald eagle typically constructs its nest near the tops of strong trees, using large sticks woven together, wedged among the branches and the trunk of the tree. These nests are typically 4-5 feet in diameter and 2-4 feet deep but can be as large as 8-9 feet in diameter across and as tall as 20 feet.[6] They are capable of withstanding very strong winds and provide excellent protection for young fledglings that could succumb to predators at an early age. The golden eagle will build its nest under rocky clefts near the tops of high hills, or high mountains. When such structure is unavailable, they too will build strong nests in the tops of trees or artificial structures such as transmission towers or other communications towers. Both species command the skies around their nests and, like the Ammonites, feel secure in their choice of nest locations.

This describes the confident feeling the Ammonites had. They commanded the high ground and were familiar with their rocky terrain. No nation seemed bent on attacking them on their own territory. These attributes led them into a false sense of security which developed into a source of pride. Their pride eventually led to their downfall.

We should find comfort in the words of Moses found in Deuteronomy 32:11-12, "As an eagle stirreth up her nest, fluttereth over her young, spreadeth abroad her wings, taketh them, beareth them on her wing: So the Lord alone did lead him and there was no strange god with him". This passage provides us with additional insight into the function of the eagles' wings and its nesting habits. In the context of this passage we find a beautiful description of the protection the Lord provided his faithful servant Jacob. That protection and instruction is figurative of the means in which the adult eagle unselfishly provides for her young. After hatching, the adult eagles are vigilant in their efforts to feed, protect, and teach their young. The long, broad, powerful wings provide protection to the chicks from any and all predators. Subsequently we see the parents feeding their young, preparing them for flight, and constantly providing them with guidance and support. Once they have acquired flight capabilities, young eagles learn to hunt by observing their parents. Those that can follow the example of their parents will survive, but those who do not will fail. While the context is focusing on the faithfulness of Jacob, the application made here can apply to all obedient saints as well. What reassurance to us that the Lord provides such guidance and protection to those who resolve to follow his will.

We find many other passages where inspired writers make mention of eagles in both the Old and New Testaments. Read and study them in view of the biological characteristics described in this chapter. Having greater knowledge of the eagle's physical capabilities, characteristics and behaviors will lead to an increased understanding of those passages. This increase in understanding should lead to a better application of God's word, and subsequently assist us in leading more holy lives.

Sources cited:

¹ The Fastest Birds in the World, Golden Eagle, World Atlas, www.worldatlas.com

² Sutton, C.; Dunne, P.; Sibley, D. (1989). *Hawks in Flight: The Flight Identification of North American Migrant Raptors.* Boston: Houghton Mifflin Harcourt.

³ Armstrong, Amy M., Facts on Eagles' Eyesight, animals.mom.me

⁴ Wolchover, Natalie, 2012, *What if Humans Had Eagle Vision*, Live Science

⁵ Armstrong, Amy M., Facts on Eagles' Eyesight, animals.mom.me

⁶ Eagle Nesting and Young, www.nationaleaglecenter.org

Sources consulted:

Grambo, Rebecca L., 1999, *Eagles*, Voyageur Press, World Life Library

Pigs

by Kevin Shurtleff

"...and the sow, after washing herself, returns to wallow
in the mire."
(2 Peter 2:22)

My dad loved pigs. I don't remember a time growing up when we didn't have pigs. It was from watching a veterinarian working on our pigs when I was in first grade that I was introduced to a profession that would shape the rest of my life.

Pigs are messy. They're smelly. They're destructive, stubborn, loud, fast, smart, cute, tasty, and in the long run, worth the trouble. It's understandable to have a love/hate relationship with pigs, but I find it hard to relate to a society without them.

For Jews, pigs were, and are, unclean. Leviticus 11:7-8, and Deuteronomy 14:8 make clear that they were not to be eaten and their carcasses were not to be touched. The reason given was although they have cloven hooves, they don't "chew the cud." In other words, they don't have the same type of digestive tracts as the clean animals with split hooves. They have a single, simple stomach, not the multiple stomachs of ruminants like cows, sheep, and goats. Their stomachs are really similar to ours. That's why a lot of research on human medicines and surgeries that have to do with our stomachs takes place on pigs.

Pigs' stomachs are similar to ours because our diets are similar. We're both omnivores. We can eat, and get the benefits of, both plant and animal material. Unfortunately, pigs are not as discriminating about what they eat as we are. Their willingness to eat dead animals and feces are probably what landed them on the unclean list.

Jews are not the only religious group that avoids pork. Muslims, Seventh Day Adventists, and the Ethiopian and Eritrean Orthodox Churches also have restrictions against pork. For Muslims, the Quran tells them that pork, "the flesh of pigs", is unclean in passages like surah 2:173 and 6:145. For the Seventh Day Adventists it is about avoiding pork as part of a healthier diet.[1] For the Ethiopian and Eritrean Orthodox Churches is seems to be a combination of religious and cultural taboos.[2,3]

Pigs' eating habits come with a fair amount of destruction. I remember when we would fence off an area of pasture and put pigs in it, they would eat everything. They ate the grass. They ate the bushes. They would use their snouts to dig up the roots of the plants and eat them. They would eat earthworms. They would eat grub worms. They would eat anything in that area that they could. When they finished "clearing" the area after a few days it would look like you had tilled the whole space and picked it clean.

Their destructive foraging habits are why people try to eradicate feral hogs from an area. They use their hard snout, strong neck, low center of gravity, and strong leg muscles to act like a plow when turning over dirt to find things to eat. The USDA estimates that feral hogs cause over one billion dollars in damage to crops and land across the country every year.[4] In Psalm 80:13, when the psalmist compares Israel to a vine, he uses the wild boar as an image of destruction upon it for good reason! Pigs wreak havoc wherever they go.

They also demonstrate their destructive habits in digging wallows. These holes start out as a way for the pigs to get down to cool, moist dirt to lay in. Then they serve to collect and hold rainwater, which is even better to cool themselves in.

Pigs are very prone to overheating. The thick layer of fat over their body serves as insulation, and this is helpful in cold weather, but makes it a challenge to stay cool in hot weather. Another problem for them is, while they do have some sweat glands[5], they lack enough to help much in the cooling process. They depend on other methods of evaporative cooling to take the place of perspiration. They wallow.

By coating themselves with water, or mud, they can cool themselves as the moisture evaporates. The mud has the added benefits of serving to protect light colored skin from the sun, and ward off some of the biting insects that can bother them.

These wallows that develop in a pig's area are used repeatedly. So in 2 Peter 2:22 when it says a sow returns to wallow in the mire after washing, it shouldn't surprise anyone. She finds comfort in the muck and mire and she's going to continue the dirty habit because she doesn't have anything else to replace it with. It's all she knows. If you provide her with a water mister, fogger, or air-conditioned building, she'll choose them, but in their absence, she's going to do what she's familiar with and wallow in the mud. It should serve as a lesson to us that people coming out of the world and sin need to replace the sin they have sought comfort in with something else. Otherwise they're likely to go right back to it when they face trials. We need to help them see better alternatives to rely on and to find comfort in.

Farmers sometimes place rings in pigs' noses to try and curb some of their rooting behavior. This does help because the metal ring causes some degree of pain when the pig pushes against it while digging. It doesn't interfere with their eating feed or softer foods, just in pushing against something harder like dirt or wood.

We know that ancient civilizations placed rings in cattle and horses noses to lead them, or for restraint, because we see it depicted in their artwork. We don't know how far back the practice of putting rings in pigs' noses goes, but it probably wasn't what prompted the reference to a gold ring in a pig's nose in Proverbs 11:22. The pig in this passage is being used because of her ugly, dirty, unclean image.

Nose rings were an adornment for women at the time like Rebekah in Genesis 24:47, or as used in Isaiah 3:21 and Ezekiel 16:12 of adornments from the Lord for His bride. So the Proverb is making the point that when a beautiful adornment is given to a pig, it doesn't negate her vices or cover up the fact that she's still a pig!

The use in Proverbs is not that different from the use in Mathew 7:6 where it mentions casting your pearls before swine. Both passages use the pig because it was considered disgusting, ugly, unclean, and one of the lowest animals the Jews knew. In a similar way, the state of the prodigal son in Luke 15:11-32 is depicted by placing him on equal footing with the swine and therefore in the lowest state possible. The Matthew passage also brings out another characteristic of pigs and that's aggression.

Pigs will fight among themselves to establish a social order. Sometimes these fights can even be deadly. Prime triggers for fighting would be when two groups are mixed together, or when a new member is added to a group. The wounds from fighting usually aren't too bad, but sometimes if one pig doesn't run away, or can't get away, the fighting goes on long enough to cause exhaustion, heat stroke, and even death.

While most pigs would rather run away when faced with danger, sometimes they will attack. Boars and sows with piglets are especially prone to charging when confronted. All pigs will bite, and in addition, boars develop tusks that they can use very effectively for slashing. While pigs are not always thought of as aggressive, they are very smart and learn how to get their way by biting. One of the main reasons people get their pet pigs spayed and neutered is to try and curb the pet's aggression.

You may wonder why Jesus would come across a herd of two thousand pigs in Mark 5:13 if they were so despised by the Jews. It was because the area on the southeast side of the Sea of Galilea was part of an area known as the Decapolis, or 10 cities. This area was heavily influenced by Greek and Roman culture in the first centuries BC and AD. The cities mentioned in the parallel accounts of Matthew 8, Mark 5, and Luke 8 were Gera and Gadar, and would have been part of this region. The majority of people in this area would have been Gentiles and therefore pork eaters. Jesus uses the opportunity of the demon possessed man to show His authority among these people. Mark 5:20 tells about the formerly possessed man going throughout the Decapolis telling what Jesus had done.

The pigs in this account are mentioned as running down a hill and drowning in the sea. Pigs can run fast, especially over short distances. That's one of the reasons a greased pig chase was ever a thing. The fact that the pigs drowned wasn't because pigs can't swim, because they can. It could have been because of the chaos of all of them piling on top of each other in the water, or because of the demons they had in them affecting their ability to control themselves.

Pigs make up important parts of the Bible even though they were looked down on and considered unclean. The Scriptures use animals like pigs that the people were familiar with to make important points. Points that are important for us to understand also. Even something like a pig that was considered despised can help us see truths about both physical and spiritual life. Surely you can make a silk purse out of a sow's ear!

Sources cited:

[1] www.adventist.com

[2] www.catholicsandcultures.org

[3] www.ncbi.nlm.nih.gov/pmc/articles/PMC4597829

[4] www.aphis.usda.gov/aphis/ourfocus/wildlifedamage/programs/nwrc/researchareas/SA_Feral_Swine

[5] Lehman, A. D.; *Diseases of Swine 5th Edition*, p. 76; Iowa State University Press, 1981.

Lions

by Ken Osborn

"And one of the elders said to me, 'Stop weeping; behold, the
Lion that is from the tribe of Judah, the Root of David, has
overcome so as to open the book and its seven seals.'"
(Revelation 5:5)

The lion, often referred to as the King of the Jungle, is both
beautiful and ferocious. While we are all likely familiar with at
least some aspects of lions, let's explore some of the characteristics
(i.e., biology, habits, etc.) of lions and see how the Bible uses those to
teach us valuable lessons not only about God Himself but also about
Satan. We will also examine the characteristics of lions that we as
humans should emulate in our lives while at the same time those we
should avoid.

Lions are the second largest member of the genus *Panthera* of the
family *Felidae*, behind only tigers in size and weight. Among the
members of *Panthera* or "big cats," lions have some unique physical
and behavioral characteristics. Male lions possess a mane which
differs from all other members of the genus. Lions also are the only
species in the genus which live together in groups called prides.
Prides are composed of a varying number of females (lionesses) and
their young (cubs). In some prides adult males live with the pride.
At other times they remain somewhat isolated for the majority of the
time. There are male lions which live as solitary nomads while others

form a group with up to three mature males called a coalition. As a coalition they defend their territory which contains one or more prides of females. While there are many factors that determine the size of a pride and the presence or absence of males full-time, food availability and competition seem to be the main ones.

Historically, modern day lions are known to have existed in Africa, the Middle East and Asia. Some now extinct species were known to live across Europe, North America and Central America.

The most recent classification of modern lions recognizes two subspecies genetically:

1. *Panthers leo melanocharta*, which are lions of southern and eastern Africa

2. *Panthers leo leo*, which are lions of central and west Africa and Asia

For our purposes we will utilize the older but more common designation to refer to African (#1) and Asian (#2) lions.

The adult African male lion typically measures about four feet tall at the shoulders and about six feet in length from the head to the base of the tail. The length of the tail varies between 26-40 inches. The average weight of the male African lion is about 420 pounds. The adult Asian male lion is somewhat smaller measuring about three and a half feet tall at the shoulders and about five and a half feet in length from head to the base of the tail. The tail length is generally comparable to that of the African male lion. The average weight of the Asiatic male is about 370 pounds. Physical differences in appearances between the two subspecies include a more prominent mane on the African male lion and a more prominent tuft of hair on the tip of the tail in the Asiatic lion. The Asian lion also has a fold of loose skin running lengthwise underneath its body which is generally absent in the African lion. Lionesses tend to be somewhat smaller than the corresponding male in both subspecies.

Historically, the habitat of the African lions ranged throughout Africa. Today, however, it is primarily in pockets throughout the sub-Saharan portion of Africa. Historically, Asiatic lions had a broad range from Northern and Western Africa through the Middle East, over into parts of Asia and through parts of southeastern Europe. Today the Asian lion is exclusively found in India in the province of Gurjarat in and around the Gir Forest National Park.

From the Bible as well as other sources we know that lions were present in both the Old and New Testament periods in the lands of the Bible. Many of the ancient civilizations mentioned in the Bible from Mesopotamia and extending down into Egypt created their deities with characteristics of the lion. Bastit, a war god of the Egyptians and the Sphinxes (which have a lion's body with a man's head) are two examples. This symbolic use of the lion is seen on down through history from its use by the Romans of New Testament times even until today where it remains the national animal and symbol for a number of nations including England.

Mosaics and figures of the lion were present in the Temple (1 Kings 7:29, 36). They are also notably prominent in Solomon's throne room where not only were there lions of gold standing beside the arms of the throne but there were also statues of lions on either end of the six steps leading up to the throne. Of that throne it is said in 1 Kings 10:19-20 "...nothing like it was made for any other kingdom." The use of the lion in these settings evoked awe at the power and majesty conveyed by this great beast which is "mightiest among the beasts" (Proverbs 30:30).

Notable characteristics of the lion throughout history include their superior strength, boldness, ferocity, regal appearance and stealth. The Bible alludes to the power and ferocity of lions by its very mention of the fact that lions killed men in the Old Testament including a disobedient prophet (1 Kings 13:24-25) and the foreigners who were sent to settle in Samaria by the Assyrians who "did not fear the

Lord" (2 Kings 17:25). Lions capability for killing men is further seen by their use as a method of executions by both the Babylonians and their successors, the Medo-Persians. The well-known story of Daniel in the den of lions (Daniel 6:16-24) points out that not only did Daniel recognize his deliverance was by the intervention of God but also King Darius realized it. When the King had Daniel's accusers thrown into the lions' den (Daniel 6:24) they were killed before "they reached the bottom of the lions' den." This statement is consistent with how lions often kill—by breaking their prey's neck.

To further illustrate the ferocity of lions, a more recent incident occurred in 1898 in Africa. The Uganda Railway was being built to link parts of Uganda with Kenya. During a nine-month period it was reported that two adult male lions, called the Tsavo Man Eaters, stalked and killed some one-hundred thirty-five workers oftentimes snatching them out of their tents at night. While that number was probably greatly exaggerated, it shows the cunning and power of the lion. The terror that these lions created delayed the completion of the railroad for over a year. Even today reports of lions killing people either in the wild or in captivity are occasionally heard.

One of the most terrifying sounds for someone who is not in a secure enclosure is the roar of the lion. It is both a declaration of power and a warning for other predators to not trespass into its territory. As the prophet Amos said (Amos 3:8) "the lion has roared who will not fear." The roar of a lion can be heard up to five miles away and can reach a volume of 114 decibels (comparable to the volume of a modern-day rock concert). This frightening sound is possible because of God uniquely designing the vocal box among some of the big cat family and is most prominent in the lion.

In accounts of both Samson (Judges 14:5-6) and David (1 Samuel 17:34-37) killing a lion is recognized as being accomplished by God's power, not their own. In verse 33 of Hebrews 11, commonly referred to as the Hall of Faith, the writer mentions "stopping the mouth of lions" as one of the acts of faith worthy of note. During the latter part of the first century, the Roman Caesars Nero and Titus made a spectacle of throwing not only criminals but also Christians to lions or other wild beasts as a form of entertainment in the Forum and later in the amphitheaters in what was proclaimed and advertised as "Damnatio ad Bestias" or condemnation to beasts.

As the Romans used the fear of lions to enforce their power and authority, the Bible also uses the lion as a symbol to illustrate power and authority. Proverbs 19:12 and Proverbs 20:2 describe the anger of a king and the advisability of being wise enough not to provoke his wrath. On the other hand, the Bible uses the lion to show the foolishness of the one who avoids doing anything profitable for fear. Proverbs 22:13 presents a hyperbole of one so lazy he would use the remote possibility of a lion being in the street to avoid doing what he should.

Additionally, the lion is seen in scripture as a description of personal enemies. The Psalmist cried out in a number of the Psalms about his despair in the presence of enemies which were more powerful than himself (Psalm 7:2; 17:11-12) and perhaps most famously in Psalm 22:12-16. There are also multiple references to despair in the presence of an overwhelming nation coming against Israel such as in Joel 1:6.

However, behind all of apparent cause for despair, the Bible makes it abundantly clear that God is the ultimate power. God used the nations as a lion against His people for judgment (Isaiah 5:26-29) but regardless of the seeming power of an enemy, God is greater (Isaiah 31:3-5). He can and will use His awesome power like a lion against all nations who fail to submit to Him (Jeremiah 25:30-38).

The Psalmist cried in despair but in the end when he looked to God he saw deliverance. In the 22nd Psalm, David sees his enemies as "strong bulls of Bashan" and as "ravening and roaring lions." Conversely, in hope of triumph, he says God can rescue him from the "power of the dog," "from the mouth of the lion" and from the "horns of the wild oxen." It is profoundly fitting that this Psalm is alluded to at Christ's crucifixion where the darkest hour of human history was soon followed by the most glorious event—the resurrection of Christ, all by the power of God (Romans 1:4).

The lion is also used symbolically to describe Satan (1 Peter 5:8). "Be sober minded; be watchful. Your adversary the devil prowls around like a roaring lion seeking someone to devour." Notice the lion-like attributes:

1. **Satan is called our adversary.** Just as the lion is not a domesticated house cat but rather ferocious and deadly, Satan is also deadly spiritually and not our friend.

2. **Satan prowls around.** Lions on the hunt are constantly searching for weakness, such as the young or the infirm. Satan is likewise looking for our weaknesses.

3. **Satan is like a roaring lion.** Just as the roar of a lion elicits fear, Satan uses pressures and intimidation to try and cause us to become fearful and lose heart.

4. **Satan is seeking someone to devour.** Satan often sugar coats sin to make it sound appealing, but his ultimate goal is to bring us down with him. Paul said in Romans 6:23, "the wages of sin is death".

Also notice the cautious approach we are to have. We are warned to be sober minded and watchful. It would be foolhardy to walk in carelessly and without protection into a lions' enclosure, likewise we should avoid exposure to Satan as much as possible. In the course of my career as a veterinarian, I have experienced some limited interaction with big cats but never without realizing their potential for inflicting serious injury or death. I even have a story about myself that involves an encounter with one of the "big cats." I was slapped by a "sedated" tiger while placing an intravenous catheter. Thankfully the extent of my injury was a massive bruise on my arm.

Despite the Devil's lion-like attributes, he can be resisted just as Paul proclaimed in Romans 8:31, "If God is for us, who can be against us". Just as Daniel and David were in the presence of lions we can be "firm in our faith" because God Himself "will restore, confirm, strengthen and establish us" (1 Peter 5:8-9).

When God is on our side there is NO power greater. This is clearly seen in Proverbs 28:1 and Micah 5:7-9 "like a lion among the beasts of the forest, like a young lion among flocks of sheep which if he passes through tramples down and tears and there is none to rescue". As noted by Paul (2 Timothy 4:16-18) he was "rescued by the lion's mouth" and brought "safely into His heavenly kingdom."

Finally, in conclusion, I draw your attention to one other mention of the lion in scripture. When John in his vision in Revelation 5 thinks no one can open the scroll held in God's own right hand, John breaks down and begins to weep loudly until an angel tells him there is one who is worthy. The angel proclaims the conqueror, one from the tribe of Judah, the root of David can open the book and calls him the Lion. However, when John turns, he sees not a Lion (a fearsome beast before which one would cower) but a sacrificial lamb.

The profundity of this vision is overwhelming. Our God is not one-sided as men through the ages have too often thought of Him. He is not the vengeful lion who waits for man to slip and fall and gleefully pounces on His prey. Nor is He a lamb so complacent that when His creature rebels against Him He suffers in silence but will reward him anyway.

Our Lord and our God has attributes reflected in being not only an awe-inspiring lion in His majesty, power, and potential for wrath, Christ is also the lamb—meek, lowly and sacrificed willingly for us (Romans 11:22).

Not only does the Godhead have qualities reflected in His various creatures, the kingdom inhabitants are also seen in this light. Isaiah, the prophet, speaks of the kingdom in which "The wolf will dwell with the lamb, and the leopard will lie down with the young goat, and the calf and the young lion will feed together, and a little boy will lead them. Also, the cow and the bear will graze, their young will lie down together, and the lion will eat straw like the ox." "They will not hurt or destroy in all my holy mountain" (Isaiah 11:6-7, 9).

In Psalm 104, which exalts God's creation, the writer states in verses 20-22, "You make darkness and it is night, when all the beasts of the forest creep about. The young lions roar for their prey, seeking their food from God." Dr. Larry Bustetter (M.S., M.Ed, EdD.) a dear friend, a faithful man of God, a microbiologist and an educator has pointed to verses 24-25 of this Psalm in some of our many conversations about God and His creation, "In wisdom you have made them all and the earth is full of Your possessions. There is the sea great and broad in which are swarms without number animals both small and great." From his unique perspective he rightly proclaims that not only the "great animals" but even down to the microbial level God's wisdom in all His creation is seen.

The poem of Cecil Francis Alexander, "All Creatures Great and Small", says in part

> All things wise and wonderful
> All creatures great and small
> All things wise and wonderful
> The Lord God made them all.
> He gave us eyes to see them
> And lips, that we might tell
> How great is God Almighty
> Who doeth all things well

Dogs

by Stewart Coffman

2 Kings 9:30-37

Nose to the ground, he dug in the fetid refuse outside the city searching for any morsel to take away the pangs of hunger when through the morass of smells the slightest vestige of raw scent hit his olfactory nerve. Blood. Fresh blood. Nose up now to catch the wide scent cone, he moved at a trot casting side to side homing in on the source. As he ran, he noted others of his pack also drawn to the scent moving in the same direction. Through the streets they raced oblivious to the curses and sticks thrown at them by the men they rushed past. His heart rate increasing, saliva pooling, now in a flat out run as the scent cone narrowed, he hit the square skidding to an abrupt halt having to dodge the hooves of the horses as they trampled the source of the scent. As the horses moved away the deformed body lay in the square, blood oozing from its wounds and scattered over the stones and walls. The pack hesitated, expecting to be attacked and driven away by the men but instead they rode away leaving the body and the hungry pack alone in the street. The pack did not hesitate.

The story of Jezebel's death in 2 Kings 9 is a fitting illustration of how canines are depicted in the Bible. The dogs of the Bible bear no resemblance to Fifi on your lap or to Duke curled in front of your fireplace. Certainly, Jews did not regard them as "man's best friend." Routinely used as a curse and derogatory term, we'll look in more detail at the imagery of dogs in the Old and New Testaments as well as investigate the different roles dogs played in surrounding civilizations and Israel. Finally, after gaining a deeper understanding of these animals, we'll look at a well-known story in the New Testament and see if perhaps we've misinterpreted the dog's role in this passage.

While not listed as ritually unclean animals in the Old Testament, Israelites may have treated them as unclean due to other factors. Certainly, as in the story of Jezebel and with the instruction given in in the old law (Exodus 22:31) to feed livestock mangled by wild animals to dogs, contact with corpses and dead animals would have communicated uncleanness to the dog (1 Kings 14:11; 16:4; 21:19, 23-24; 22:38; 2 Kings 9:10, 36; 1 Kings 21:23). Though the Old Testament description of dogs is oftentimes as wild packs of scavengers, mention of dogs in Job and Isaiah indicate that they were used as watch dogs or guard dogs due to their ability to bark and warn their masters (Job 30:1, Isaiah 56:10-11).

Numerous places in the Old Testament the term dog is used derogatorily to indicate scorn or lowliness (Deuteronomy 23:18; 2 Samuel 3:8; Proverbs 26:11; Ecclesiastes 9:4). When used to express personal humility or unworthiness it is oftentimes immediately preceded by the word "dead" as if to indicate that the person was even lower than a dog (2 Kings 8:13, 2 Samuel 9:8; 1 Samuel 24:14). Probably the most emphatic use in the Bible of this derogatory label was by Goliath in his rage at the egregious insult to him by the Israelites sending the youth, David, to face him with a staff and sling, "Am I a dog, that you come to me with sticks?" (1 Samuel 17:43).

In 1935, a trove of letters was found in Lachish, some 30 miles southwest of Jerusalem, written to the commander of the garrison at Lachish just before Nebuchadnezzar's invasion of Judea in the 6th century BC. The letters describe specific maneuvers by the Israelites in preparation of the coming battles and interestingly, include a self-deprecating notation from the writer when he addresses the Lachish commander and refers to himself in closing as "Who is your servant but a dog."[1]

While the term in Deuteronomy 23:18 has been cited as a reference to a male prostitute, there is considerable evidence that dogs were used in pagan healing rituals and the phrase "the wages of a dog" may indicate tainted money obtained from pagan worship that should not be used in payment for a vow to God just as the fee of a prostitute should not.[2]

Domestication of canines occurred several thousand years ago but the Israelites seemed to be slow adopters until the intertestamental times. While not a part of the scriptures, a 2nd century BC work entitled the Book of Tobit indicates dogs had entered the Jewish family space. In this story, the author begins the narration with Tobias beginning a journey accompanied by his pet dog.[3]

In the New Testament, the family dog is the powerful metaphor used by the Syrophoenician woman urging Jesus to heal her demon-possessed daughter: "Yes, Lord, yet even the little dogs eat the crumbs that fall from the table of their master" (Matthew 15:27; Mark 7:28). The first written collection of Jewish oral traditions known as the Mishnah, written during the first and second centuries, contains rules about when a master is responsible for their pet dog biting another's livestock,[4] the requirement to chain a dog in order to raise it in a house,[5] and even an argument between two rabbis about whether the dog should be considered a wild or a domestic animal.[6]

Despite the adoption of dogs as family pets and work animals by this time, the term was still used derogatorily in the New Testament both as a comment to a person's low social status (Matthew 7:6; 15:26) and as a comment to their being evil (Philippians 3:2; Revelation 22:15).

There is solid evidence by the fourth millennium BC of human and canine companionship in the ancient Near East. Hunting dogs appear on numerous pieces of early Egyptian and Assyrian artwork. Domesticated dogs have been uncovered in the destruction layers of ancient Jericho, located in what is now the West Bank region, from the Neolithic period (modern archaeologists place settlements there as far back as 10,000 BC), and over 700 hundred purposefully buried dogs were uncovered at the coastal city of Ashkelon from the Persian period (550-330 BC).

During the Persian period, Ashkelon benefitted from significant cultural diversity, including Persians, Egyptians, Phoenicians, and Greeks, so it is difficult to determine exactly who buried the dogs. None of the other items found during the excavation indicate why they were buried with such care and no temple or shrine has been found near the site. They appear to be buried in the same pose and no signs of trauma were noted to the skeletons. While the burial site remains a mystery, it is clear the dogs were held with some regard.[7]

Egyptians had a close relationship with canines, employing them as companions, hunting animals, and even deity. A limestone pottery fragment dating to around 1100 BC, found near Tutankhamun's tomb displays the Pharaoh spearing a lion with a hunting dog at his side. The pottery text reads, "The slaughterer of every foreign land, the Pharaoh—may he live, prosper, and be healthy." This fragment is currently on display at New York's Metropolitan Museum of Art. Dogs in Egypt were also associated with the jackal-headed god of the underworld, Anubis. Cult centers to the god Anubis have been excavated and thousands of mummified dogs have been found inside them.[8]

While the Jews may have been slow to see the benefits of domesticated canines, Greeks and Romans were the opposite. Homer's Odyssey (eighth century BC), makes several references to domestic dogs. When Odysseus returns from his decades-long journey, Argos, the faithful dog he left behind, dies of joy when he recognizes the scent of his missing master. This same passage may also be the first reference to the "doggy bag:" "As when dogs fawn around their master as he comes from a feast, for he always brings them bits to delight their hearts."[9]

We are largely familiar with the ancient canine's role of hunter, guard dog, and pet. However, the dog also had a connection to the healing arts. Ancient authors noted, for example, that the dog knows that it should elevate an injured leg, knows what plants to eat as medicine to induce vomiting, knows to remove foreign bodies, and that the dog instinctively knows to clean their wounds by licking them.

The saliva of dogs was even regarded mystically in ancient times. In Egyptian magical papyri, there are several spells that describe a dog's saliva as being venomous, due to the resulting pain and swelling from a dog bite. We now understand this reaction is due to the local inflammatory response and even infection at times due to specific bacteria like *Pasteurella multocida*. Interestingly, the cure, according to the ancient tomes, requires more dog saliva.[10]

The association of dogs and healing is also reflected in the cult of Asclepius, the god of medicine in Greek mythology. One of the oldest and most widely known *asclepeion* (healing temple) was started in the 4th century BC in southern Greece. This cult grew very popular and pilgrims flocked to their temples for hundreds of years during the intertestamental and New Testament times. Not only would non-venomous "sacred snakes" slither around the temples to cure visitors, the temples housed sacred dogs that would approach the visitors and heal them by licking their wounds. One such reported cure from the fourth-century BC Epidaurian Tablets reads: "A dog cured a boy from Aegina. He had a growth on the neck. When he had come to the god, one of the sacred dogs healed him—while he was awake—with its tongue and made him well."[11]

So, while the Old Testament is consistent in its low characterization of dogs and the New Testament Jews still regarded these animals as lowly, the impact of Greek, Roman and other surrounding cultures on Jews in the first century may give us a clue to understanding the story of the rich man and Lazarus from Luke 16 more completely.

This deeper understanding makes a great difference in our reading of this story. In Luke 16:21, Lazarus lies there at the gate, and "longs to satisfy his hunger with what fell from the rich man's table, and even the dogs would come and lick his lesions."

Traditionally, the function of the dogs licking Lazarus has been described as a sign of extreme misery. He is apparently so weak and ill that he cannot drive away these "unclean" animals who are feeding off him.[12] Given our improved understanding of the times though, it is more likely that the dogs would have been viewed positively in this situation by a first-century audience as a sign of caring by the rich man's pets, not mistreatment. In fact, the irony that Lazarus is being cared for by lowly dogs and not the aloof, pompous rich man, would not have been lost on the readers of this text who undoubtedly would also be familiar with the similar irony found in the parable of the Good Samaritan in Luke 10. Indeed, the irony goes even deeper when you pause to ponder for a moment that the last detail we learn of Lazarus before he dies is that his wounds are being licked by the dogs' wet tongues and the first request in Hades by the rich man is that he begs Lazarus for a drop of water to wet his own tongue.

Dogs played an interesting and graphic role in the Bible. From derogatory epithet to house companion to caring nursemaid, the canine's role and status certainly changed over the thousands of years represented by the scriptures. Our perception has historically been a negative one, but archaeology and other ancient writings seem to be begging us to reconsider the biblical role played by man's best friend.

Sources cited:

[1] Dennis Pardee et al., *Handbook of Ancient Hebrew Letters*, SBL Sources for Biblical Study 15 (Chico, CA: Scholars Press, 1982), pp. 67–114

[2] Biblical Archaeology Review 17:3, May/June 1991

[3] Tobit 6:2; Tobit 11:4

[4] Baba Kama 5:3

[5] Baba Kama 7:7

[6] Kil'ayim 8:6

[7] Crawford, John S. "Caleb the Dog," *Bible Review* 20.2 (2004): 20, 22, 24, 26–27

[8] Patrick F. Houlihan, "Canines," in *The Oxford Encyclopedia of Ancient Egypt*, vol. 1, ed. Donald B. Redford (Oxford: Oxford Univ. Press, 2001), p. 230

[9] Homer, *Odyssey* 17.290–327

[10] Egyptian Demotic Papyri xiv.554–562

[11] Friedrich Hiller von Gaertringen, ed., *Inscriptiones Graecae, IV. Inscriptiones Argolidis*, 2nd ed. (Berlin: De Gruyter, 1929)

[12] Justin David Strong, "Lazarus and the Dogs: The Diagnosis and Treatment," *New Testament Studies* 64.2 (2018), pp. 178–193

Deer

by Mark Bailey

"As the deer pants for the water brooks,
so pants my soul for You, O God."
(Psalms 42:1 NKJV)

Perhaps the verse in the Holy Scriptures most often associated with the deer species in all of the text. I believe that is so, due to our familiarity with the song, "As the Deer," by Martin Nystrom, arranged by R.J. Stevens. It is a beautiful hymn and one that well conveys the sentiment of the Psalmist and his yearning for a right relationship with the God of heaven. A yearning that is especially intense during times of trial, tribulation, while cast down, and reproached (Psalms 42:3, 5, 9, 11). There are times in our lives that test us severely; yet for those that love the Lord, there is the confidence within us that God is our rock (Psalms 42:9) and not even death itself can separate Him and His love from us (Romans 8:31ff). We need Him like no other and as the thirsty deer pants for the refreshing sips of cool water from a brook, you and I must also "thirst" for His righteousness (Matthew 5:6); and realize that only His Son can supply us with "living water" (John 4:10). Earthly water sources provide temporary refreshment; Jesus provides that which is eternal and will never run dry (John 4:14).

The Psalmist brings to mind the scene of a deer panting, desperately needing water to sustain its very life. A truth for all wild things from a biological point of view; they need food, cover, water. Of the three, water is the most necessary. Survival without the other two can be sustained for a short period of time. Not so without water.

Depending upon the location the Psalmist is considering, water may not have necessarily existed in abundant supply. Much of Palestine is relatively arid; thus, the reference to the deer "panting" for the refreshment and hydration it found at the brook.

Antarctica and Australia are the only continents in the world that do not have at least one deer sub species roaming the land. Deer are members of the family *Cervidae*, a family of the class *Mammalia* or mammals. Yukon moose are considered to be the largest members of the deer family, while Northern Pudu are generally accepted as being the smallest and are found at high elevation in the Andes Mountains of Columbia, Ecuador and Peru. Perhaps the white-tailed deer of North America comes to mind whenever the word "deer" is mentioned, but it is unlikely the Psalmist is referencing that sub-species. Your mental image of a deer depends upon what part of the world you reside in. They are virtually everywhere.

Because they are so abundant, and present since the creation, deer have likely been a food source for mankind since the post-diluvian days of Noah and his descendants.

> "So God blessed Noah and his sons, and said to them: 'Be fruitful and multiply, and fill the earth. And the fear of you and the dread of you shall be on every beast of the earth, on every bird of the air, on all that move on the earth, and on all the fish of the sea. They are given into your hand. Every moving thing that lives shall be food for you. I have given you all things, even as the green herbs'" (Genesis 9:1-3; see also 10:8-9).

Deuteronomy 14:5 lists the deer as a "clean" animal, one suitable for the children of Israel to consume. For those of us that hunt deer species, we appreciate the sport of pursuing them; but we really appreciate them as outstanding table fare! Solomon included deer in the daily provisions for those that resided in his house on a daily basis; "ten fatted oxen, twenty oxen from the pastures, and one hundred sheep, besides deer, gazelles, roebucks, and fatted fowl" (1 Kings 4:23).

A quick glance of that impressive list would lead the reader to conclude that deer meat or venison was literally "fit for a king" from a culinary standpoint. Venison was a major food source in colonial North America and uncontrolled market hunting severely decimated deer populations all over the United States around the turn of the twentieth century.

Visionaries like Teddy Roosevelt and others saw the need to control and regulate the harvest of these magnificent creatures in North America. With sound game management practices in place, deer numbers are thriving and are likely at an all-time high in numbers in many parts of the United States.

White-tailed deer are the most popular big game species in this country and in some states, can be hunted five and six months out of the calendar year. Deer hunting is big business, too. In 2011, the National Shooting Sports Foundation conducted a study on the spending of deer hunters in the state of Wisconsin. Approximately 615,000 plus hunters spent $2.17 billion directly and perhaps as much as $3.4 billion indirectly on the beloved sport!

Let us always remember though, that the biological traits of deer species all over the world are God's business. He alone has given them their unique anatomical, physiological and reproductive traits.

"Do you know the time when the wild mountain goats bear young? Or can you mark when the deer gives birth? Can you number the months that they fulfill? Or do you know the time when they bear young? They bow down, they bring

43

forth their young, they deliver their offspring. Their young ones are healthy, they grow strong with grain; they depart and do not return to them" (Job 29:1-4).

"The voice of the Lord makes the deer give birth, and strips the forests bare; and in His temple everyone says, 'Glory!'" (Psalms 29:9)

Many a deer manager and hunter has vainly attempted to solve the deer behavior riddle without success. The research and energy resources directed towards these magnificent creatures continues to expand.

It is not coincidental, in my opinion, that deer have captivated the attention of both admirers and hunters since the beginning of time, not to mention those who seek venison solely for its impressive culinary rewards. I have often wondered if Isaac's request of Esau, Genesis 27:3-4, and the "savory dish" he craved on his death bed involved venison. In a wild setting the deer sub-species as a whole are beautiful and magnificent creatures; both pleasant to look at and athletically gifted. They are marvelously camouflaged, though most are wearing coats predominated by solid colors. The males, and in some cases females, sport headgear that is both attractive to a prospective mate and suitable for combat. Mississippi State University recently conducted a study on white-tailed deer that suggested does preferred bucks with larger antlers. White-tailed deer are capable of speeds up to 35 mph, though they cannot sustain that speed for long, and are capable of vertical leaps of seven feet from a standing start and perhaps as high as ten feet from a running start. When describing the future glory of Zion as it compares to the spiritual desert of Edom in Isaiah 34, Isaiah speaks of the lame leaping "like a deer" in Isaiah 35:6:

"Then the lame shall leap like a deer, and the tongue of the dumb sing. For waters shall burst forth in the wilderness, and streams in the desert" (Isaiah 35:6).

The deer sub-species of the world are as elusive as any big game species on the planet. They are crepuscular, i.e., generally active at daylight and after sunset. The Lord has blessed them with great vision, superb hearing and an outstanding sense of smell. Though they don't see some colors well, their ability to detect movement in a 270 ft. plus radius makes visual detection of potential predators easy. Their sense of smell may be 500 to 10,000 times more acute than a human's. Deer can sort out odors that are ten days old. More "brain power" is devoted to sense of smell than the other senses in these wily creatures. I have been "busted" by a deer's olfactory prowess on numerous occasions and from a considerable distance.

Generally speaking, the deer species that North Americans are familiar with are very adaptable to environment, ecosystem, or habitat change. They can thrive in a variety of settings, urban agricultural, tropical, forested, prairie and even desert habitats can and do support various subspecies of cervids. Yet, in every ecological niche or climate they must have the necessities of life; food, water, and shelter (cover). All living must have those things, else life ceases. As we consider our eternal destiny and, in light of a whole host of passages that deal with the spiritual nourishment that only comes from God thru His Son, let's consider one final "deer" passage.

> "And from the daughter of Zion all her splendor has departed. Her princes have become like deer that find no pasture, that flee without strength before the pursuer" (Lamentations 1:6).

Jeremiah here laments the dire circumstances of God's children. The city of Jerusalem and the southern kingdom finds itself reduced to rubble by the Babylonian invasion. Judgment had been prophetically promised by the prophets on God's people because they had been unfaithful, idolatrous, and rebellious. He was no longer "with" them, and a remnant was carried away to Babylonian slavery. Jerusalem is in ruins, physically and spiritually and Jeremiah paints a word picture, comparing the rulers to a deer that lacks the necessities of existence and fleeing from predators. It is a grim sight, and one we must learn from. Without the spiritual sustenance and protection supplied by God Almighty through His Son, you and I are just starving and weakened deer, fleeing from our adversary, the devil.

May we learn to "pant" for the living water the Savior so graciously and bountifully offers.

Sheep

by Rob Perkins

"The LORD is my shepherd; I have all that I need.
He makes me lie down in green pastures, he leads me
beside quiet waters, he refreshes my soul. He guides
me along the right paths for his name's sake."
(Psalm 23:1-3)

This Psalm is one of the most beloved of all Psalms. It came out of the heart of David who as a young lad shepherded sheep and who in his maturity shepherded the nation of Israel. It majestically portrays David's humility and dependency upon God as a shepherd—his personal shepherd.

Howdy! My name is Rob Perkins. I am a 1981 graduate of the Texas A&M University college of Veterinary Medicine. For the first 30 years of my practice career I have been involved in large animal medicine which of course included the care of small ruminants like sheep. In addition, I shepherd a congregation in Corpus Christi, Texas.

First let's define some terms. Rams are male sheep of breeding age. Ewes are female sheep of breeding age. Lambs are male or female sheep whose growth plates have not closed (ossified) yet. The way that is determined is at the time of slaughter. Pressure is applied on a long bone at the growth plate, and if it breaks, the growth plate has not ossified, and the animal (meat) is classified as lamb. If the "break bone" does not break, then the meat is classified as mutton which has a lesser value.

Sheep have great economic value. The price of a lamb on today's market is about $100 and some flocks have 1,500 animals. The math says that's a flock that's worth $150,000 in today's dollars. Sheep are produced for meat, wool, dairy products, lanolin and sacrifice (in the Jewish economy). Generally you need one ram per 15 to 20 ewes for breeding purposes. That means you sell most of your male lambs and retain the female lambs for future breeding stock.

Raising sheep during Bible times, and until the general use of fencing, was much different than it is today. Before fencing, sheep were "free" grazed over thousands of acres of land and needed to be closely monitored by human beings. In fact, shepherds lived with the flock of sheep and developed a close human/animal bond. A flock of sheep managed by one shepherd could number about 1,500 head of sheep. Today most land is privately owned with sturdy fences to both contain them and protect them from predation, and it requires much less human oversight.

In fact, the best documented model for raising sheep might be demonstrated in the mid to late 1800s in south Texas. Land was plentiful, labor was cheap, and compared to cattle, sheep are more easily handled. The handling of cattle requires cowboys (and cow horses), roping skills and pens. A single sheep can be handled by one human being with little help.

"In one, often called the partido system, sheep owners hired individual herders to tend the animals. Customarily, herders and owners entered into contracts as to the length of service and wages. It was common for the sheepherder to tend about 1,500 sheep. He remained with them day and night, moved them from range to range, and participated in lambing, shearing, and other activities associated with sheep raising. At the end of the term of the contract the herder received his wages, took a brief respite from the range, and subsequently entered into a new contract."[1]

As you might expect, the life of a shepherd could be very lonely with minimal human contact. It was a lonely life.

Robert Adams went to work when he was 16 in 1863 tending sheep near Casa Blanca. He wrote that he did not see the inside of a house for two years and didn't see people sometimes for two or three months.[2]

Imagine the shepherd boy David who probably didn't see another human being for months, using the days of solitude to develop other skills. Perhaps the skill of playing a musical instrument, the composing of songs, the ability to use a sling and of course meditation and prayer to his creator. These skills may never have been developed if young David had access to a hand-held electronic device and the internet.

> "One of the servants answered, 'I have seen a son of Jesse of Bethlehem who knows how to play the lyre. He is a brave man and a warrior. He speaks well and is a fine-looking man. And the Lord is with him.' Then Saul sent messengers to Jesse and said, 'Send me your son David, who is with the sheep.' So Jesse took a donkey loaded with bread, a skin of wine and a young goat and sent them with his son David to Saul" (1 Samuel 16:18-19).

Genetics is important in the raising of sheep. Wool that is uniformly white is more valuable than that of sheep who are spotted. The white wool has more consistent staining characteristics. That's why you see Jacob offering Laban (his father-in-law) to keep only the spotted sheep. He was acting humbly by asking for the inferior quality lambs. Of course God blessed him for his humility, and we know how that turned out.

"'What shall I give you?' he asked. 'Don't give me anything,' Jacob replied. 'But if you will do this one thing for me, I will go on tending your flocks and watching over them: Let me go through all your flocks today and remove from them every speckled or spotted sheep, every dark-colored lamb and every spotted or speckled goat. They will be my wages'" (Genesis 30:31-32).

So, genetically speaking, a wise shepherd would select rams that are uniformly white and will produce uniformly white lambs. Of course the ram is only responsible for 50% of the genetics, but it is a 50% that is easily controlled. If, after lambing season, spotted lambs are produced then a different ram can be brought in. If only a few lambs are born spotted, then the ewe probably needs to be culled.

In addition, a wise shepherd would select for sheep who produce twins or even triplets. When those animals are identified, special care in the form of nutrition and protection would be provided. A ewe who for whatever the reason fails to produce a lamb every year is culled and sent to the market.

Besides wool and wool quality, sheep also are selected for meat characteristics. So there are wool-type sheep, meat-type sheep and sheep who have both characteristics. Generally speaking whichever area the market is strongest for places a demand upon the shepherd to satisfy that market. In today's world the wool market is declining due to the abundance of other types of fiber: cotton and synthetics.

Sheep do not have great defense mechanisms against predators. They don't have fangs, claws, significant horns or brute strength. Generally speaking the best defense for sheep in the face of a predator is to circle up with all the young sheep in the center and the more mature sheep on the perimeter. Often times a predator will back down in the sight of a united front and wait for a better day when a lamb, for instance, might stray away from the safety of the flock and the oversight of a shepherd.

"Keep watch over yourselves and the entire flock of which the Holy Spirit has made you overseers. Be shepherds of the church of God, which He purchased with His own blood. I know that after my departure, savage wolves will come in among you and will not spare the flock. Even from your own number, men will rise up and distort the truth to draw away disciples after them. Therefore be alert and remember that for three years I never stopped warning each of you night and day with tears" (Acts 20:27-28).

Sheep producers today, and presumably in Bible times, utilize animal guardians to protect their sheep. Canine breeds like Anatolian shepherds and great Pyrenees are raised so they "bond" with the sheep and live with them 100% of the time. Additionally some producers used donkeys in the same pastures with sheep to protect them. These types of animals live with the sheep 100% of the time and are extremely effective at limiting predation. On a personal note, I employ a half-Anatolian, half-Great Pyrenees to protect our chickens. I have observed that if a hawk flies too low, our dog will chase it.

Our sheep practice consists of some herd health but is primarily the raising of lambs by high school students for showing in county fairs. The bulk of the problems with those kind of lambs was parasitism, urinary tract problems associated with feeding grain based diets, respiratory disease, gastrointestinal disorders, castration complications and injuries (primarily lacerations).

Sheep are designed to graze in native pastures which would include grasses and shrubs. In certain landscapes they are preferred over cattle who only forage on grasses. When producers start feeding grain-based diets for the purposes of producing a lamb who might score well, problems are incurred. One devastating condition a lamb can have is grain-diet-induced bladder stones, which do not occur in lambs who are allowed to free graze. Those small stones can lodge in the urethra and cause blockages. Urine builds up until the bladder cannot hold any more urine. There is back pressure on the kidneys causing uremia and an extreme amount of pain. Sheep love to eat grain-based diets but are not designed to do so.

During the course of my study on this topic, I wrote the following five articles on my blog about how these concepts about sheep interact with Bible teaching.

Lessons from Sheep: Defense!

In the Bible, God's people are often referred to as a flock of sheep, and those in charge of God's sheep/church are called shepherds or pastors. There are probably a lot of reasons for describing the church as a flock of sheep, but one very important reason is because sheep depend upon each other for defense.

Sheep don't have fangs or claws like a lion. They aren't swift enough to outrun a wolf. They can't spray repulsive scent like a skunk, and they can't camouflage themselves. So what can they do? In the wild they can group together in a solid circle with the rams and older animals on the periphery and the younger and weaker in the interior. A solid front can be intimidating to a predator, and the predator may skulk off waiting until an unsuspecting lamb wanders off from the protection of the group to acquire his prey.

Of course domestically, a flock of sheep has a shepherd who is constantly vigilant watching out for the flock; so too the church. Just as flocks gather together to ward off predators, Christians congregate together and strengthen each other by learning about God, learning how to lead sin-free lives and by learning what it means to live a life of service until faith is built up and fortified.

Once faith is mature and the soldier of Christ is fully armored, the great lion Satan will skulk away in fear, especially if he is facing an army of Christian soldiers.

Remember what Jesus told Peter? "Upon this rock I will build my church and the gates of Hell shall not prevail against it."

There are a lot of reasons to congregate together with other Christians and defense is one of those—even sheep know that.

Lessons from Sheep: Value

In the Bible, the Lord's people have been compared to a flock of sheep and their leaders are called shepherds. God owns the flock, and the shepherds are accountable to him. One of the reasons for the comparison is that sheep have value and so do the Lord's people.

Sheep produce meat, dairy products, wool and lanolin, etc. The shepherd finds the best pastures for the sheep so that their nutritional needs are met and they can be productive. He also protects them from predation. The shepherd may also vary the genetics of his flock by bringing in rams who have the characteristics he desires (wool vs. meat types). Frequently a ewe may produce twins or even triplets. The shepherd identifies sheep with superior genetics and maximizes their impact in the flock. If a ewe doesn't produce a lamb every year, she is culled—as are the aged sheep. Every year the shepherd gives an accounting to the flock owner.

The Lord's people/church has great value. Her pastors/shepherds nourish the flock by teaching from God's word. They are also taught to congregate/flock with each other. There is no culling of the aged in the church. The aged can still provide sound judgment and opportunities of service and honor for the rest of the congregation.

Those who possess superior spiritual genetics, if called upon, will sacrifice their own lives for the benefit of another. The church's spiritual economic value is the good deeds she does for each other and for the community. The goal of the pastor/shepherd is to deliver the entire flock/church to their owner (God) on the Day of Judgment, and that's exactly what God expects of them. Don't let God down.

Lesson from Sheep: Nutrition

The nutritionally wise shepherd leads his flock to pastures that offer the very best nutrition. Sheep are herbivores. They are designed to eat grass but can also browse on brush. In fact sheep and goats are sometimes used to control brush in pastures.

In the show lamb business, lambs are fed grain-based diets to develop the kind of body condition that will impress show judges. As a veterinarian, we see problems associated with feeding lambs a primarily grain-based diet. It is not uncommon to attend a sick lamb who has developed bladder stones and suffered a urethral obstruction that is potentially fatal. Sheep are not designed to eat grain-based diets, and as a consequence suffer from various metabolic diseases (chronic pancreatic inflammation, kidney disease, lamenesses and obesity). Sheep love to eat corn, sorghum and all kinds of grains—it's like eating candy for them. So too the church/flock.

Wise shepherds feed their flock with a balanced diet of God's word. Too many shepherds and churches focus on things like:

- Fighting the denominations. The bulk of teaching in these type of congregations focuses on what's wrong with other churches.

- Social things. Some churches minimize Bible teaching and focus on fun things—activities and eating and sports and the like.

- Bible study. Some churches' overwhelming focus is Bible study to the exclusion of anything social.

- The positive aspects of God—His love, grace and care for His people to the exclusion of accountability and punishment.

- The negative aspects of God—His hatred of sin and punishment and destruction to the exclusion of His mercy and forgiveness.

God's people need the right nutrition—a comprehensive balanced diet of God's word and the social things that naturally follow from that understanding. An awful lot of teaching is soft and tastes good (like candy) but can lead to spiritually crippling and sometimes fatal spiritual disease.

Watch out for congregations whose sheep wander off and no one seems to care and whose sheep are spiritually weak and diseased. If you want to be the right kind of Christian, look for a congregation whose shepherds are wise, who care about their sheep, and whose sheep are spiritually sound and happily flock together. The proof is in the pudding.

Lesson from Sheep: Conflict Between Shepherds

> "And there was trouble between the shepherds of Abram's livestock and the shepherds of Lot's livestock...and Abram said to Lot, 'Please let there be no trouble between you and me and between our shepherds and for we are brothers. Isn't the whole land before you? Please separate from me and take first pick and I will go the opposite direction'" (Genesis 13:7-9).

Abraham's and Lot's shepherds were having problems with each other. Sometimes the Lord's shepherds have problems with each other too. The problem with problems is that if they are not resolved, and not resolved in the proper manner, relationships and the flock/congregation can be harmed, sometimes irreparably. Maybe we can learn a few things from Abram and Lot.

Abraham communicated with Lot, he didn't ignore the issue. The life blood of a congregation is effective communication. A lack of communication especially between shepherds can make the problem worse. In congregations, shepherds should never make any kind of decision without first consulting the other shepherds, even if it's something as simple as what color to paint a classroom. That sort of communication, even at its simplest and most basic level, begins forming the basis for trust.

Notice that Abraham, in his wisdom, saw the direction things were headed with Lot and took steps to prevent it before lasting harm was done. Abraham reminded Lot that they were "brothers." The importance of that relationship cannot be overstated. The basis for every relationship is trust. If a husband and wife don't trust each other they aren't going to have a very good marriage, and if a congregation's shepherds don't trust each other then nothing can be accomplished. Congregations are a reflection of their leadership.

Abraham in his humility told his nephew Lot to pick whatever land he wanted, and he would take whatever Lot didn't want. Shepherds in a congregation should subject themselves in humility to each other, when possible. It's hard for a relationship to go sour if a pattern of subjection has been established. When some sort of crisis arises in a congregation (and it will), if her shepherds have complete trust in each other, they can focus all their strength and energy in overcoming it.

Abraham greatly valued the livestock (wealth) that God had given him. He also valued his relationship with his nephew Lot, whom he called a brother. In his humility he allowed Lot to take the best pasture lands. Because of his humility God blessed him with much more wealth.

Shepherds in congregations likewise should value the sheep they have been placed in charge of, and they should also value their fellow shepherds. Shepherds don't always have the same abilities. Some are better at teaching, some are better at hospitality, some are better at sharing their wealth and some are better at communication, etc.

It would be a mistake to de-value your fellow shepherd because you think your abilities are better than theirs. The proper attitude is to be thankful for your fellow shepherds and appreciate the different abilities that they have. Like Abraham, shepherds in the Lord's church should constantly be looking for potential problems and should treat fellow shepherds as "brothers".

Remember a few milliliters invested in prevention is far less costly than a liter invested in a cure.

David, the Shepherd Boy Who Would Become King

From his youth David shepherded his father's flocks of sheep. In all probability he carried his camping equipment on a cart. He would build his own fire, cook his own meals and clean up after himself. His father would send him supplies from time to time. Shepherds might spend months to years away from towns and town life.

During the day he watched the sheep graze all day long and cared for all their needs. Undoubtedly he helped the ewes deliver their lambs, helped clean them up, assisted them in learning how to nurse and whatever else they needed.

During his free time he became an expert with a sling and could kill (with a stone) an eagle that might prey upon a baby lamb. Those sling-propelled stones could also fend off and kill larger predators like wolves, coyotes, lions, etc. David also in his hours of being alone learned to play musical instruments and compose songs. Those songs were sung to his audience of sheep to calm them down when needed. David also spent a lot of time looking at nature and contemplating God, praying and singing songs of praise to him.

David learned to be shepherd of Israel by shepherding sheep. He understood how to take care of God's flock of people and see to their needs. He killed the Philistine giant Goliath who was threatening God's flock Israel with a sling-propelled rock to the head just like he had done many times before when predators threatened his sheep.

David sang to his people about God and wrote poetry about the God he had learned about while tending sheep. Nature is a great teacher.

When David was off in those faraway pastures grazing sheep, he had no idea he would one day be king of Israel (and no one else did either), but God knew. You may think you have the smallest and most insignificant job in the world, but set your eyes and the course of your life on God because God can do great things with humble people.

Sources cited:

[1] https://tshaonline.org/handbook/online/articles/aus01

[2] https://www.caller.com/story/news/2018/10/15/rise-and-fall-sheep-era-south-texas/1617990002

Serpents and Snakes

by Mark Bailey

"Now the serpent was more cunning than any beast
of the field which the Lord God had made. And he said
to the woman, "Has God indeed said, 'You shall not eat
of every tree of the garden'?"
(Genesis 3:1)

Very few, if any, of the members of the animal kingdom are viewed with the level of disdain and fear with which snakes and serpents are viewed. How many movie watchers remember the scene in *Raiders of the Lost Ark*—Indiana Jones peering down into dimly lit ruins after uncovering the hidden rooftop access, only to discover that the floor below is covered with snakes? "Snakes. Why did it have to be snakes?" he mutters. This is the view of the majority of folks when it comes to these slithering members of the reptile family.

Snakes are elongated, legless, carnivorous reptiles of the suborder *serpentes* and are found on every continent of the globe with the exception of Antarctica. They are found on smaller land masses as well, with a few notable exceptions—Iceland, Greenland, Ireland, New Zealand, and the Hawaiian Islands are all devoid of serpents. There are some 3,600 different species of snakes; of which approximately 725 are venomous and only 200 of those being capable of harming or fatally injuring a human being with one bite. Most venomous snakes use their venom to subdue or kill prey rather than for self-defense. Non-venomous snakes kill their prey by constriction or swallow their prey alive. Because of flexibility in their mandibles, all snakes are capable of swallowing prey up to three or more times the width of their skulls!

Serpents come in a variety of sizes and colorations, from the tiny Barbados thread snake at four inches long, to the reticulated python which may grow to 23 feet or longer. Some are brilliantly colored, while others are masters of concealment and camouflage. The green anaconda is considered to be the heaviest snake on Earth, weighing in at a whopping 215 pounds in some cases. Snakes are covered in scales, and their skin usually has a very smooth, dry texture. Specialized scales on their bellies allow them to "grip" surfaces and propel their bodies along in serpentine fashion. Periodically they shed their scales/skin or molt in a process called ecdysis. They shed their complete outer layer of skin in one layer, sort of like turning a sock inside out.

All serpents use their sense of smell to track potential prey, and some have infrared-sensitive receptors that allow them to sense the radiant heat of warm-blooded potential victims. Snakes smell by using their constantly active forked tongues to collect airborne scent particles. They pass the particles they collect to the Jacobson's organ or vomeronasal organ located in pits just above their mouths to be evaluated. A snake's underside is also very sensitive to vibration, allowing them to sense approaching prey or danger. They can feel the faintest of vibrations in the ground.

Snakes are cold-blooded ectotherms, which means that they have little to no physiologic capability of controlling their body temperature. They rely on environmental heat sources to regulate their temperature. In environments where temperatures fluctuate and winters can become seasonally cold, snakes bromate, which means they are awake but sluggish and inactive.

Most snakes lay eggs after mating to produce progeny, but a few species bear living young. Those that lay eggs usually abandon the clutch shortly after the laying process is completed; however, some species like the king cobra construct nests, lay their eggs, and then remain in close proximity to their clutches until they hatch out. Pythons actually coil around their eggs to incubate them.

Culturally, serpents have played a significant role in the history of mankind in several countries. Genesis 3:1 portends of that observation and fact. Snakes are considered acceptable and even exquisite table fare in some countries. Smoked rattlesnake is available in some Walmart grocery aisles! They are considered to be great, low maintenance pets by some; mostly because they require nourishment every 5-14 days in many cases and are relatively inactive otherwise. Captive snakes have been known to live in excess of forty years! Serpents are a part of religious worship and symbolism in some parts of the world. In the United States, especially in Appalachia, some Pentecostal groups believe that Mark 16:18 calls them to handle venomous snakes (pit vipers) to prove their faith and trust in God.

> "And these signs will follow those who believe: In My name they will cast out demons; they will speak with new tongues; they will take up serpents; and if they drink anything deadly, it will by no means hurt them; they will lay hands on the sick, and they will recover" (Mark 16:17-18).

These words were spoken by Christ concerning the miraculous works that believers in the early church would be capable of. Now that the completed canon of God's word has been delivered unto mankind, the miraculous is no longer necessary to confirm faith (1 Corinthians 13).

It is quite possible that the Savior's words in Mark 16 are prophetic concerning a very specific event recorded for us by Luke in Acts 28:3-5. The apostle Paul was shipwrecked on the island of Malta while travelling to Rome to appeal to Caesar. Evidently he gathered up a pit viper while acquiring fire wood, and after placing the bundle on the fire, the venomous snake struck him on the hand and remained there while Paul withdrew his hand. Onlookers view Paul as a capital offender and that the deadly bite is justice being served, but Paul shakes off the serpent and miraculously suffers no ill effects.

Hindu worship involves the symbols and even live specimens of Nagas or cobras in an annual festival called Nag Panchami. In India, commonly referred to as the land of the snakes, serpents are worshipped and seen as symbols of fertility. Snakes are one of 12 celestial animals of the Chinese Zodiac in the Chinese calendar. Ancient Greeks viewed the serpent as a symbol of healing, and the medical world continues to use three different symbols involving snakes to this day. The Bowl of Hygieia, symbolic of pharmacy, the Caduceus and Rod of Asclepius, symbolic of medicine, all have snakes playing a major role in the composition of those symbols.

Obviously snakes have influenced the history of mankind from the very beginning, as is evidenced by our introduction to the serpent in Genesis 3: 1-2, 4, 13-14. The serpent's role in the deception of Eve (1 Timothy 2:14) forever altered the course of mankind, both physically and even more so spiritually.

This chapter will not dedicate much verbiage to a debate of whether Satan occupied a snake's body in the style of demons possessing swine (Matthew 8:28-32) or if miraculously the prince of the power of the air transformed himself into a serpent's form. Readers are called upon to determine for themselves concerning the matter, and it is a discussion that many have taken up in the past and likely will in the future as well. Also intertwined in that debate is the matter of whether snakes and serpents were originally upright animals and capable of communication with humankind prior to Genesis 3:14. Were either or both capabilities literal, or were they manifestations of Satan's immense power and deceptive methods? The text does not elaborate or reveal the answers, and therefore we must be content to examine God's word from that perspective.

What I do know in regard to the passage found in Genesis 3:13-15 is that all members of the serpent family were cursed by God as an outcome of the role the serpent played in the deception of Eve and the resulting choice to succumb to temptation and commit sin by both Adam and Eve.

> "And the Lord God said to the woman, 'What is it that you have done?' The woman said, 'The serpent deceived me, and I ate.' So the Lord God said to the serpent: 'Because you have done this you are cursed more than all cattle, and more than every beast of the field; on your belly you shall go, and you shall eat dust all the days of your life. And I will put enmity between you and the woman, and between your seed and her Seed; He shall bruise your head, and you shall bruise His heel'" (Genesis 3:13-15).

Regardless of the serpent's previous circumstance in regard to anatomy and ambulatory methods or status, they would now and forevermore crawl on their bellies and be cursed (loathed) more than any other beast on the planet. This is the general consensus concerning snakes today. Genesis 3:15 is directed toward Satan primarily and is the very first Messianic prophecy on record—thus the beginning of both realms, physical and spiritual (heavenly), anticipating the Christ of God coming to Earth to conquer sin and death. Though Satan was the deceiver and liar in the process, all of serpent-kind paid a severe penalty in this instance. Snakes were cursed by God and therefore the basis for mankind's continued disdain for and loathing of these belly-crawling reptiles. Most of us have heard the old saying, "The only good snake is a dead snake." That mindset is pervasive and perhaps only rivaled by our fear and dread of spiders. As you might imagine, biblical references to snakes are negative or convey some sort of warning in the context.

Genesis 49:17

"Dan shall be a serpent by the way, a viper by the path, that bites the horse's heels so that its rider shall fall backward" (Genesis 49:17).

Jacob prophetically proclaims the future for all of his sons in chapter 49. Dan is likened unto a "serpent by the way" and a "viper by the path," likely a reference to opportunistic positioning for a surprise attack or strike. He is one that will prey on those that pass by unawares and target any vulnerability, striking at the heels of passing steeds so as to cause chaos and ultimately upending the rider. Jacob is perhaps referencing his son's willingness to lie in wait and strike out on an unsuspecting helpless victim, wreaking havoc in the process. Judges 18 comes to mind, when the children of Dan dealt ruthlessly with a defenseless, quiet and secure Laish.

Exodus 4:1-3

"Then Moses answered and said, 'But suppose they will not believe me or listen to my voice; suppose they say, "The Lord has not appeared to you."' So the Lord said to him, 'What is that in your hands?' He said, 'A rod.' And He said, 'Cast it on the ground.' So he cast it on the ground, and it became a serpent; and Moses fled from it" (Exodus 4:1-3).

Most of us are familiar with this Bible story and Moses' rod miraculously turning into a serpent, confirming that Jehovah had sent him to speak on behalf of heaven's throne. True to form, Moses ran when God transformed his staff into a snake! The miraculous transformation is repeated in Exodus 7:8-13 when Aaron cast the rod down in the presence of Pharaoh and his court. Through magic and enchantments, Pharoah's magicians seemingly replicate the feat, only to watch in amazement and horror as Aaron's rod swallowed up all of theirs, thus hardening Pharoah's heart.

Numbers 21:4-9

In Numbers 21, during the 40 years of wandering in the wilderness, the children of Israel were restless and complaining because of the circuitous route that Moses was leading them on to avoid Edom. As a result of their murmuring and speaking against God and Moses, God sent "fiery" serpents to afflict and punish the people (Numbers 21:5). Many were snakebite victims and died as a result (Numbers 21:6). Upon their confession of sin, the people requested that Moses intervene as an advocate and pray on their behalf. God instructed Moses to fashion a likeness of the fiery serpent, place it on a pole, and bite victims were to look upon the object and live.

> "Then the Lord said to Moses, 'Make a fiery serpent, and set it on a standard; and it shall come about, that everyone who is bitten, when he looks at it, he will live'" (Numbers 21:8).

It is hard to know what "fiery" means in the context of this passage. Perhaps it relates to coloration, maybe their deadly bite burned, and the possibility exists that they literally breathed fire. I'm inclined to consider the second option as a likely scenario, but much like in Genesis 3, the text here in Numbers 21 does not specify. Interestingly Jesus references this occasion in John 3:14-15 and compares the looking upon the serpent on the pole leading to saving physical lives, to the belief in Him being raised on the cross leading to eternal life. "And as Moses lifted up the serpent in the wilderness, even so must the Son of Man be lifted up, that whoever believes in Him should not perish but have eternal life" (John 3:14-15).

Ultimately, Hezekiah destroys the bronze serpent that Moses had made hundreds of years earlier because Israel had begun worshipping the image, calling it Nehustan (2 Kings 18:4).

Job 26:13

There are several references in both the wisdom literature and the prophets to serpents. Job 26:13 and Isaiah 27:1 both use serpents or the "piercing" of a feeling serpent to reference God's power, ability, and command over His creation. I've tried numerous times, vainly so, to catch a fleeing snake. Most of us, like Moses, will run in the opposite direction!

> "By His breath the heavens are cleared; His hand has pierced the fleeing serpent" (Job 26:13).

Psalms

David references liars and those that refuse to hear God in Psalm 58:3-5. The wicked are classified as liars in verse 3 and in verse 4 he proclaims: "Their poison is like the poison of a serpent; they are like the deaf cobra that stops its ear."

He speaks of evil men continually planning evil things in Psalm 140:1-3. In verse 3 he makes reference to snakes using their tongues seeking out prey. These evil men, like snakes, are constantly searching for victims.

> "They sharpen their tongues like a serpent; The poison of asps is under their lips" (Psalm 140:3).

Like the wicked in Psalms 58, these evil men are liars.

In Psalm 91:13, both the lion and the serpent (cobra) represent the pitfalls and dangers of our spiritual lives. It is a beautiful passage that is tied to the Savior's trials and temptations directly by Satan, recorded for us in Matthew 4 and Luke 4. Those that make Jehovah their dwelling place or refuge will be safe and secure (Psalm 91:9-10).

> "He shall give His angels charge over you, To keep you in all your ways. In their hands they shall bear you up, Lest you dash your foot against a stone. You shall tread upon the lion and the cobra, the young lion and the serpent you shall trample underfoot" (Psalm 91:11-13).

In Matthew 4:6 and Luke 4:10, Satan has positioned himself and Jesus on the highest elevation of the temple mount in Jerusalem.

The devil quotes Psalm 91, tempting the Savior to jump, citing verses 11 and 12. But Jesus points out quickly that there is a huge difference between a child of God falling versus jumping, so as to "test" God's faithfulness. The cobra and serpent, along with the lion, represent the spiritual dangers in this life we can only overcome if we seek refuge in the Lord. We will not overcome temptation by and through our own power.

Proverbs

The sudden, devastating effects of your blood alcohol rising are the topic of Proverbs 23:32: "At last it bites like a serpent, and stings like a viper."

The drinker feels little to no effect initially, but suddenly alcohol "bites" you, with the swiftness of a pit viper's strike! This passage goes on to describe the diminishing of normal vision, rational speech and decision making (Proverbs 23:29-35).

Again, Proverbs 30:18 gives us a laundry list of four things in this life that impress the writer from an amazement point of view or perspective:

"The way of an eagle in the air, the way of a serpent on a rock, the way of a ship in the midst of the sea, and the way of a man with a virgin" (Proverbs 30:18).

All four references are likely related to movement, navigation or control of the situation that is presented. Though I cannot be certain, I think of a snake climbing a vertical rock that is smooth, and doing so with relative ease when I read this passage. I've seen snakes climb up the side of the walls of houses, seemingly defying gravity.

Ecclesiastes

In Ecclesiastes 10:8-9, Solomon gives us some proverbial statements that deal with the dangers associated with everyday activities in the work place: digging a pit, quarrying stones, splitting wood and breaking through a wall. Breaking through barriers that conceal hidden spaces may result in an unfortunate encounter with a snake. How many of us have accidentally uncovered a snake under old lumber or underneath items stored in an old building or barn? In verse 11 of that same chapter, the wise man likens the babbler to an uncharmed snake. The babbler is guilty of "running off at the mouth" and is as dangerous as an uncharmed cobra.

"A serpent may bite when it is not charmed; the babbler is no different" (Ecclesiastes 10:11).

Isaiah

After King Ahaz died, Israel's longtime nemesis Philistia rejoices prematurely and God through Isaiah issues a stern, chilling, warning of impending judgment.

"This is the burden that came in the year that King Ahaz died. 'Do not rejoice, all of you Philistia, Because the rod that struck you is broken; for out of the serpents roots will come forth a viper, and its offspring will be a fiery flying serpent'" (Isaiah 14:28-29).

This passage prophetically speaks of the demise of the Philistines at the hands of countries likened unto serpents that gradually worsen in regards to their capability of inflicting harm. Most of the snake references in the prophets, major and minor alike, deal with some sort of judgment or affliction against the Israelites or other nations. Some reference the character of the ungodly, such as Isaiah 59:4-5:

"No one calls for justice, nor does anyone plead for truth. They trust in empty words and speak lies; they conceive evil and bring forth iniquity. They hatch viper's eggs and weave the spider's web; He who eats of their eggs dies, and from that which is crushed a viper break out" (Isaiah 59:4-5).

New Testament

In Matthew 3:7, John the Baptist refers to the religious leaders of his era, the Pharisees and Sadducees, as a "brood of vipers." Make no mistake, being called a "bunch of snakes" is no compliment! Many of us have heard someone referred to as a "snake in the grass" (remember Jacob's assessment of son Dan in Genesis 49?), and John's words concerning these men in Matthew 3 is spot on in most cases. Ultimately they would crucify the Christ of God.

Matthew 10:16 is perhaps the only "positive" reference to snakes in all of Holy Scriptures.

> "Behold I send you out as sheep in the midst of wolves. Therefore be wise as serpents and harmless as doves" (Matthew 10:16).

Jesus is encouraging His disciples to not be naïve in regards to both the ways of the world and the worldly. The snake is wary, constantly aware of his surroundings, and both the twelve and the current disciples need to embrace that trait. Snakes are masters at escaping danger, and we are to be as well.

There are a few other New Testament references to snakes. Matthew 7:10 and Luke 11:11 make the observation that human fathers, though capable of sin, won't give a child a snake when they've requested a fish for sustenance. 2 Corinthians 11:3 references the serpent of Genesis 3:1 addressing the serpent's (Satan's) craftiness and deceptive power. Paul offers this observation about his concerns for the church at Corinth and, by extension, us:

> "But I am afraid that, as the serpent deceived Eve by his craftiness, your minds will be led astray from the simplicity and purity of devotion to Christ" (2 Corinthians 11:3).

All of John's references in the Revelation are tied to Genesis 3 and point to Satan (see Revelation 12:9, 14, 15, 20:2).

"And the great dragon was thrown down, the serpent of old who is called the devil and Satan, who deceives the whole world" (Revelation 12:9a).

The Bible's references to snakes and serpents are plentiful but not flattering, to say the very least.

The scene in the Garden of Eden, the deception of Eve, the temptation presented and then the choice to commit sin by both Adam and Eve resulted in a curse on snakes. The curse still remains and will until our Savior returns. Mankind's general perception of these reptiles has perhaps softened somewhat over the course of time but not enough to really move the needle on the meter of acceptance, and so it shall always be.

Cattle

by Robert Bonner

"For every beast of the forest is Mine;
The cattle on a thousand hills."
(Psalm 50:10)

Cattle have been an integral part of this world and of society since creation. Because of their intrinsic value as food sources, beasts of burden, sacrifices, and commerce, I believe cattle are chief among all livestock discussed in the Bible. As we begin with creation in Genesis, cattle are the only species specifically mentioned. "Then God said, 'Let the earth bring forth living creatures after their kind: cattle and creeping things and beasts of the earth after their kind'; and it was so," Genesis 1:24. The Hebrew word used for cattle, *behemah*, as defined by Strong's, can denote cattle, a beast or animal. The fact that cattle are mentioned in Genesis 1 apart from other animals clearly denotes God's plan for them and their value to mankind.

In the ungodly line of Cain, only four generations from Adam, Jabal and his descendants are mentioned as the first cattlemen in Genesis 4:20. Many ancient civilizations, including Egypt worshiped cattle or the likeness of cattle as part of their idol worship. It is important to note that modern livestock practices and raising cattle is not a new concept and that mankind has been directly involved with cattle husbandry since the beginning of time.

One amazing quality of cattle is the fact that they produce a food source for people from land that would otherwise be unfit for agriculture. Land that is too rough or arid for crops can still produce grass and other plants that are digestible by the unique digestive tract of cows. The intelligent design of God's hand is evident in the cow's compartmentalized stomach system. Their forestomach acts as a large fermentation vat for various bacteria and microorganisms that digest otherwise undigestible food sources containing high levels of cellulose or hemicellulose. Cattlemen are, in essence, grass farmers using cattle to produce a valuable meat or milk protein source from otherwise unusable land. After the children of Israel defeated the Amorites on their journey toward the promised land, the tribes of Reuben, Gad, and Manasseh elected to stay in the land of Jazer and Gilead because of the vast pasture lands.

> "Now the sons of Reuben and the sons of Gad had an exceedingly large number of livestock. So when they saw the land of Jazer and the land of Gilead, that it was indeed a place suitable for livestock... '...the land which the Lord conquered before the congregation of Israel, is a land for livestock; and your servants have livestock'. They said, 'If we have found favor in your sight, let this land be given to your servants as a possession; do not take us across the Jordan'" (Numbers 32:1, 4-5).

This region is known for its hills and mountainous terrain. Even in modern agriculture, cattle are rarely found in large numbers in the flood plains as these areas are reserved for more profitable crops. As the psalmist states in Psalm 50:10, "For every beast of the forest is Mine; The cattle on a thousand hills."

Cattle husbandry practices both in Bible times and today vary with the type and age of cattle. In today's world, cattle grazing vast expanses of native forage are generally beef cows on a cow-calf operation. The calves from these cows are usually placed on a more concentrated ration or prime pasture after weaning and are finally finished on grain in a feedlot prior to slaughter. We see similar examples in Bible times of calves being fed for the sole purpose of meat consumption. In any type of meat, the distinct flavor comes from the fat therein. The fat marbled in a prime cut of meat is what makes a steak so desirable and valuable. In Luke 15:23 we read of the father preparing the fatted calf for the celebration of his long-lost son's return. In 1 Samuel 28, the witch of Endor prepared a fatted calf from within her home for Saul and his men. These calves were likely fed a concentrated diet for the same reasons as our modern feedlots feed calves today. In today's world, prime cuts of meat from a finished feedlot calf are often times reserved for special occasions such as birthdays, anniversaries, and holidays. When looking at the story of the prodigal son, the beef consumed during that celebration was no different. The father had his best robe put on his son, sandals on his feet, likely the family ring on his hand, and the fatted calf was killed. The fatted calf was extremely valuable and symbolized the most honor that the father could give the son in the form of a meal which is why the older son specifically complained about it and not the clothing or inheritance in Luke 15:28-30.

> "But he became angry, and was not willing to go in, and his father came out and began entreating him. But he answered and said to his father, 'Look! For so many years I have never neglected a command of yours, and yet you have never given me a kid, that I might be merry with my friends; but when this son of yours came, who has devoured your wealth with harlots, you killed the fattened calf for him'" (Luke 15:28-30).

In today's world, cattle have been genetically selected for either meat or milk production. Most dairy cattle are fed concentrated grain diets during lactation, and most dairies in the world are in close proximity to good farmland. Most milk references in the Bible refer to goat's milk, but there are references that let us know that mankind bred cows specifically for milk production. In 1 Samuel 6, the Philistines contemplated returning the Ark of the Covenant to Israel. After capturing the Ark as a battle trophy, the hand of God had been upon them, and He afflicted them with tumors and death and struck down the idol of their god, Dagon. As a test to see if the God of Israel was truly responsible, the priest and diviners of the Philistines chose to place the Ark on a cart with a trespass offering inside. Instead of using trained oxen or horses to pull the cart, they chose to tie two milk cows that had never pulled a cart and that had calves at home to pull the cart.

They did not guide the cows but let them lead the cart in order to test the power of God. In a normal situation, the cows would have simply pulled the cart in the direction of their calves at home and might have destroyed the cart and its contents. The willpower of a cow to return to its un-weaned calf is extremely great and there are few fences that will restrain a cow pulled away from its nursing calf. When cattlemen wean calves, they always pull and move the calves, not the cows, for this very reason. That is what makes this miracle of God so great. These lactating cows that were not broke to lead a cart guided the cart with the Ark and offering inside straightway to Beth-shemesh proving again the power of God as he directed their path (1 Samuel 6:10-12). Another example in the Bible where dairy cows are mentioned is in 2 Samuel 17:29. In David's flight from Absalom, men of the land offered him food and provisions including cheese from milk cows. "Honey, curds, sheep, and cheese of the herd, for David and for the people who were with him to eat; for they said, 'The people are hungry and weary and thirsty in the wilderness'." These scriptures show that cows were used for milking and would imply that they were kept in confinement or smaller areas at home for milking purposes.

Other cattle kept in confinement are those used as beasts of burden. This is one area in which we do not see examples in modern agriculture since the tractor has replaced the oxen and horse as the means of providing mechanical physical labor on the farm, and modern machinery is used for planting, crop harvesting, and processing. Third-world countries today still use cows to pull plows and carts. The cattle pulling the plows in the Bible were trained to follow the commands of their master. In 1 Kings 19:19-20, Elisha was plowing a field with a pair of oxen and eleven others when Elijah chose him. Cattle are intelligent and quite capable of being trained for various tasks. We see them not only pulling the plow in Bible times but also working the threshing floor.

In 2 Samuel 24, David purchased the threshing floor of Araunah with its oxen in order to construct an altar and offer the oxen as sacrifice to the Lord. Cattle were also used for transport.

> "When they brought their offering before the Lord, six covered carts and twelve oxen, a cart for every two of the leaders and an ox for each one, then they presented them before the tabernacle. Then the Lord spoke to Moses, saying, 'Accept these things from them that they may be used in the service of the tent of meeting, and you shall give them to the Levites, to each man according to his service'" (Numbers 7:3-6).

The cattle used for labor in the Bible were treated differently than pasture cattle. They were kept in stalls and fed a grain-based diet. "But the Lord answered him and said, 'You hypocrites, does not each of you on the Sabbath untie his ox or his donkey from the stall, and lead him away to water him?'" (Luke 13:15). "You shall not muzzle the ox while he is threshing" (Deuteronomy 25:4).

Another key function for cattle in Bible times was their use as animal sacrifices. The bull was chief among Old Testament sacrifices as it was the sin offering for the sins of a priest (Leviticus 4:3) or for the sin of the whole congregation (Leviticus 4:13-14). The bull used for the sin offering was to be a choice animal without blemish. "For you to be accepted—it must be a male without defect from the cattle, the sheep, or the goats" (Leviticus 22:19). In order to make atonement for himself, Aaron was to offer a bull (Leviticus 16:11). Since cattle are considered clean animals, they would have also been included in the burnt offering by Noah to God upon exiting the ark in Genesis 8:20. Under the Old Law, the bull was the chief sacrifice because of its value, yet we read in Hebrews 9 and 10 that the bloodshed in animal sacrifice was insufficient for the forgiveness of sins compared to Christ our Savior.

> "And not through the blood of goats and calves, but through His own blood, He entered the holy place once and for all, having obtained eternal redemption. For if the blood of goats and bulls and the ashes of a heifer sprinkling those who have been defiled, sanctify for the cleansing of the flesh, how much more will the blood of Christ who through the eternal Spirit offered Himself without blemish to God, cleanse your conscience from dead works to serve the living God?" (Hebrews 9:12-14)

> "For it is impossible for the blood of bulls and goats to take away sins" (Hebrews 10:4).

Cattle are more valuable than other forms of livestock today and in Bible times because of several factors. They are the largest type of livestock. Cows often weigh 1,100 pounds; bulls can weigh over 2,000 pounds, and finished calves at the feedlot will weigh 1,200 pounds. Cows consume more forage, and it takes more input to raise a calf. On the same area of land used to raise one cow, about six sheep or goats could be easily sustained. The gestation period of a cow is about nine months, and she is usually able to have only one calf per year. The gestation period for sheep and goats is only five months, and they sometimes kid or lamb 1.5 times per year and often have twins. Cows are not generally mature until around fifteen months of age and do not have their first calf until two years of age. Often sheep or goats are having their first babies by one to one and a half years of age.

Cattle have defined the wealth of individuals or cultures for ages and have been an important part of agricultural commerce since the beginning of time. Cattle were an important part of the wealth of Egypt as they worshiped the Apis Bull which many believe was the inspiration for the golden calf worshiped by Israel in Exodus 32. The number of oxen are used to define the wealth of Job in Job 1:3 and 42:12. Abraham was very rich in cattle (Genesis 13:2), and David appointed men to oversee his cattle in 1 Chronicles 27:29. Even in today's world, as the wealth of a nation increases, its consumption of beef increases as well.

We see cattle having an impact on everyone in the time of the Bible. It is because of this that we see so much imagery and symbolism used with cattle as the subject. The yoke symbolizes a burden placed on man in many scriptures. In 1 Kings 12, the people asked the new king, Rehoboam, to make the yoke which his father Solomon put upon them lighter. The people used the yoke to symbolize the tax burden or labor force required by King Solomon. Rehoboam responded in verse 14 after listening to the council of the young advisors and said, "My father made your yoke heavy, but I will add to your yoke." In the prophecy of Christ's crucifixion in Psalm 22:12, those crucifying Jesus are referred to as "strong bulls of Bashan." When he was discussing financial support of an evangelist in his work, Paul quoted scripture saying in 1 Corinthians 9:9, "For it is written in the Law of Moses 'You shall not muzzle the ox while he is threshing.' God is not concerned with the oxen is He?" Finally, we have the symbolism of the opportunity before us to serve and labor for the Lord. "Take My yoke upon you, and learn from Me, for I am gentle and humble in heart; and you shall find rest for your souls. For My burden is easy, and My load is light'" (Matthew 11:29-30).

We see the imagery of cattle throughout the Bible, in both the Old and New Testaments. We can appreciate the strong tie between cattle and society in both Bible times and the modern world. As we study these amazing animals, we see God's hand in their design and in their purpose for mankind.

(All scripture references are from the New American Standard Bible.)

Goats

by John Allen

"All the nations will be gathered before Him, and He will separate them one from another, as a shepherd divides his sheep from the goats. And He will set the sheep on His right hand, but the goats on the left."
(Matthew 25:32-33 NKJV)

This earth, God's magnificent creation, can only be seen as a design by a higher divine authority, if one is honest with logic. The complexities of nature and things found on this earth can only be done by a creator and not by some random happenings. The Bible, written by inspired men, explains to us how this earth came into being. There is no other logical explanation known to man.

All throughout the Bible, God used animals, plants, insects and other things in nature to help us have a better understanding of the things around us to grasp the points being made. These were used as metaphors, similes and analogies.

During the time that the inspired writers penned the books of the Bible, the people were an agrarian, or agriculture, based society. The people were living close to nature and had a deep dependence on agriculture products for survival. They lived close to nature and could understand points being presented when animals, plants, insects and other things in nature were used as examples of like points.

Today, we too are dependent on agriculture for survival, and even though a large percent of the population isn't as close to nature as they were in Biblical times, we too can have a better understanding with these examples, when we explore them closely. "For since the creation of the world His invisible attributes are clearly seen, being understood by the things that are made, even His eternal power and Godhead, so that they are without excuse" (Romans 1:20).

As Job was being criticized and mocked, the Word states, "But now ask the beasts, and they will teach you, and the birds of the air, and they will tell you, Or speak to the earth and it will teach you, and the fish of the seas will explain to you. Who among all these does not know that the hand of the Lord has done this" (Job 12:7-9). God clearly intends for us to have a better understanding of His Word by using the things we can see and know in his creation.

There are over 210 breeds of goats in the world and approximately 450 million goats around the world today. In addition to this there are many crosses of these breeds. Various breeds of goats serve different purposes.

There are breeds of goats whose fundamental purpose is for meat production. Others are primarily for milk production, while others produce fiber that can be spun and used for cloth, curtains, rugs or clothing. As a result, goats are very important for food and fiber production around the world.

Goats were some of the earliest domesticated animals and were managed by shepherds in herds. This could insure the regular supply of meat, milk and fiber. In addition, the hides or skins were used for many purposes to help sustain certain essentials of life. Goats were some of the earliest animals domesticated by humans for agriculture production due to their varied and numerous uses. Goat remains have been found at archaeological sites in Jericho, Choga Mami, Djeitun and Cazonu, dating the domestication of goats in Western Asia to between 8,000 and 9,000 years ago.

Goat breeds come in many sizes and colors. They can be solid colored, multi-colored or spotted. These colors are usually white, black, brown, tan or a mixture of these. Most of the Palestinian and Syrian sheep are white, whereas most of the goats are black. The major contributor of modern goats is the Bezor , or Ibex goat which is distributed from the mountains of Asia Minor across the Middle East to Sind. The Bezor is sometimes referred to as being in the goat antelope family, and is believed to be one of the main ancestors of the modern domestic goat. They include a wide range of species that live in many extreme environments, from deserts to mountainous regions. These goats tend to form groups or herds with others of the same species. They usually have ashy colored coats with dark stripes along their spine.

Both males and females are horned with the male exhibiting a very striking set of horns which curve upwards and backwards from the head in an arc shape. Many times this imagery of goat horns is used to be symbolic of the devil. This picture image of Satan is seen in many pagan devil worshipping societies. This representation of Satan as a man with a goat head is still used today in cartoons, costumes, movies and heavy metal bands. Satan worshippers today still use the image of a goat and it is prevalent in modern pop culture.

One of the most popular images of a Satanic goat dates back to the Knights of Templar, who were accused (some say falsely) of worshipping an idol known as Baphomet. Baphomet has been sketched as a winged man with the head of a goat. The pagan worship of gods with goat qualities date to before the time of Christ.

In Greek mythology, Pan is considered to be one of the oldest of Greek gods. He is associated with nature and is said to prefer to live in wooded area and pasturelands. Typically the worship of Pan was in rural areas far from populated cities. Pan was considered the patron god of the Arcadia region. The appearance of Pan was half-goat and half-man. The bottom half of his body was like a goat, including hooves, with the top half looking more like a man; however, he is depicted with horns like a goat. Pan possessed enormous strength, could run for long periods of time and was impervious to injury. He could also transfer objects into different forms. Shrewdness and humor were portrayed in his personality. He played a flute made of reeds lined together, which is where the pan flute originated. He was a wild, frightening, unbridled creative force of nature. This mythological false god with many qualities of goats was important in ancient history and the imagery obtained from goats and their nature. It is believed that this mythology began before the time of Christ and was passed down through oral tradition.

Goat diets are varied, depending on the environment which they inhabit. They will eat brush or browse (vegetation such as twigs, tender shoots and leaves of trees and shrubs), grass or forbs, but they prefer the brush or browse. In many regions, these brush species are higher in protein, thus enabling goats to thrive in harsh environments. This diet is somewhat different than sheep, which prefer grass or forbs.

Both goats and sheep are receptive to internal parasites which can cause extensive health problems. Because of their grazing habits of eating more brush up off the ground, goats are less prone to these internal parasites than sheep that graze more on grass or forbs close to the ground. Sheep tend to become infested by ingesting the parasites' eggs on the ground. This factor helps goats thrive and remain healthy in harsh environmental conditions such as desert lands better than sheep.

Goats have been an important food source for people for thousands of years. Even today, goats remain an important food source all over the world. There is some debate as to what animal constitutes the most red meat consumed worldwide; however, it is agreed that goat meat ranks toward the top in worldwide consumption. Goats were considered clean animals to eat under the Mosaical law under the conditions outlined in Leviticus 11.

"These are the animals which you may eat: the ox, the sheep, the goat. The deer, the wild goat, the mountain goat, the antelope and the mountain sheep" (Deuteronomy 14:4-5).

Goat milk was a very important part of the diet of people in Biblical times, with many goat herds raised primarily for their milk and cheese production. It is also known that goat milk is highly digestible and nutritious. "You shall have enough goats' milk for your food. For the food of your household, and the nourishment of your maidservants" (Proverbs 27:27).

In the Bible, goats are mentioned in passages numerous times as sources of meat and milk. Since meat from an adult male is often tough, and females are needed for replacements to increase the herd, it is the male kid goat that is often mentioned in these passages as a revered food source.

"So Gideon went in and prepared a young goat, and unleavened bread from an ephah of flour. The meat he put in a basket, and he put the broth in a pot; and he brought them out to him under the terebinth tree and presented them" (Judges 6:19).

Goat hair and skins were also utilized in making items of importance to the people for everyday uses and also for trade. Some breeds of goats have coarse hair that can be woven into a rough textured fabric or some breeds, such as the modern Angora, produce fine hair that can be woven into soft and luxurious cloth. These fibers continue to be a significant and essential agriculture industry in present time.

In Exodus we read, "You should also make curtains of goat hair, to be a tent over the tabernacle. You shall make eleven curtains" (Exodus 26:7). From this passage we learn that the curtains in the tabernacle were made of goat hair.

Sackcloth is a fabric that is usually made of coarse goat hair. It is a dark, rough and very coarse fabric that is used for sacks, and is also worn by mourners as a sign of grief, submission, humiliation and repentance. "Then Jacob tore his clothes, put sackcloth on his waist, and mourned for his son many days" (Genesis 37:34). "Then David said to Joab and to all the people who were with him, 'Tear your clothes, gird yourselves with sackcloth and mourn for Abner. And King David followed the coffin" (2 Samuel 3:31). "Then David lifted his eyes and saw the angel of the Lord standing between earth and heaven, having in his hand a drawn sword stretched out over Jerusalem. So David and the elders, clothed in sackcloth, fell on their faces" (1 Chronicles 21:16).

As Jonah preached in Nineveh, sackcloth was mentioned to be used on man and beasts during repentance. The fabric was likely very itchy and uncomfortable to wear. "But let man and beast be covered with sackcloth, and cry mightily to God; yes, let everyone turn from his evil way and from the violence that is in his hands" (Jonah 3:8).

Goat hair is also used to make tents of the Bedouin Arabs and similar dwellings in the Old and New Testament times. The hair of the goat was considered to be of importance and real value to the Hebrew people. Goat skins have always been widely utilized for leather in Bible lands. Goat skin leather is tougher than sheep skin, which is softer and can tear more easily. From ancient history to the present age, goat leather has been used for making jugs and bottles for storage and everyday use. In historic times, goat skins were used as parchment for writing and document recording purposes. "Purify every garment, everything made of leather, everything woven of goats' hair and everything made of wood" (Numbers 31:20).

In the Old Testament, goats were often used as offerings or sacrifices. In the Law of Moses, the Levitical priesthood was given exact standards by which they carried out their priestly duties. "And he shall take from the congregation of the children of Israel two kids of the goats as a sin offering, and one ram as a burnt offering" (Leviticus 16:5). These sacrifices were to be flawless examples from the flock, a valuable surrender of your possessions and livelihood that had been provided by God.

Under the Old Law, the Levitical priests had to make sacrifices each year for the atonement of the sins of the people; whereas, under the law with Christ's sacrifice, it was done once for all. "But in these sacrifices there is a reminder of sins every year. For it is not possible that the blood of bulls and goats could take away sins" (Hebrew 10:3-4).

> "Previously saying, 'Sacrifices and offering, burnt offerings, and offerings for sin you did not desire, nor had pleasure in them (which were offered according to the law) then he said, Behold, I have come to do your will, O God, He takes away the first that He may establish the second. By that will we have been sanctified through the offering of the body of Jesus Christ, once for all'" (Hebrews 10:8-10).

There are numerous passages in the Old Testament scriptures describing the offerings of goats.

Under the New Law with the sacrifice of Christ, the forgiveness of our sins is through Him, the perfect sacrifice, if we obey His commands. There is no longer a dependence on the yearly inadequate animal sacrifice of bulls and goats, with this salvation through Christ.

The mention of the use of a scapegoat under the Old Law is significant as well. On the Day of Atonement, it was required that the high priest sacrifice a goat, and then another goat would be used as a "scapegoat." Moses ordered that the scapegoat would be taken out into the wilderness to carry the sins of the people away.

> "He shall take the two goats and present them before the Lord at the door of the tabernacle of the meeting. Then Aaron shall cast lots for the two goats: one for the Lord and the other lot for the scapegoat" (Leviticus 16:7-8).

"Aaron shall lay both his hands on the head of the live goat, confess over it all the iniquities of the children of Israel and all their transgressions, covering all their sins, putting them on the head of the goat, and shall send it away into the wilderness by the hand of a suitable man. The goat shall bear on itself all their iniquities to an uninhabited land, and he shall release the goat in the wilderness" (Leviticus 16:21-22).

The term "scapegoat" is widely used in today's society. Oftentimes it is used to denote someone who is "taking the fall" or being used as an out for someone else's wrongdoing.

A "Judas" goat is another term that is widely used among goat producers and ranchers. Goats are easily trained to help lead other goats or sheep onto a truck or trailer for hauling to market or slaughter. At the slaughter plant, these Judas goats help lead goats or sheep to the killing floor. Oftentimes, goats or sheep will tend to balk, but will usually easily follow the Judas goat. This term came about from the betrayal of Christ by Judas. Thus, the Judas goat betrays the herd or flock by leading them to places they normally won't go.

Sheep and goats are often referred to together as there are many similarities. However, in their nature and attitudes there are major differences. Sheep will tend to be a lot more easily led and dependent on a shepherd. Anyone who has raised goats will relate that they have a more independent nature, and are typically more persistent and headstrong.

Grazing habits are different, in that goats will not stay as close to one another in the flock, but will spread out more on their own. They will also graze into more treacherous terrain and will graze all day. Sheep on the other hand, will lie around more. Goats are intelligent creatures. Sometimes they use this intelligence to cause destruction, more so than the docile sheep. Goats are curious by nature and are often more destructive to property and surroundings with their inquisitiveness. Goats are more aggressive than sheep and will often find any hole in a fence to escape. When predators attack, goats are known to turn and fight, which is indicative of their more aggressive nature, whereas sheep will lie down and take the consequences.

Mature male goats, called billies, are often aggressive in their behavior and have a dominant attitude with the herd. They frequently fight with each other to achieve this dominance. They can be observed to play "king of the mountain" on a small hill at an early age. With this word picture in the mind's eye, we have an imagery to compare to the writings in Proverbs:

> "There are three things which are majestic in pace, yes, four which are stately in walk: A lion, which is mighty among beasts and does not turn away from any; a greyhound, a male goat also, and a king whose troops are with him" (Proverbs 30:29-31).

Daniel 8 depicts a vision that appeared to Daniel. In this prophetic revelation from God much imagery was used with a ram and a male goat.

> "Then I lifted my eyes and saw, and there, standing beside the river, was a ram which had two horns, and the two horns were high; but one was higher than the other, and the higher one came up last. I saw the ram pushing westward, northward, and southward, so that no animal could withstand him; nor was there any that could deliver from his hand, but he did according to his will and became great. And as I was considering, suddenly a male goat came from the west, across the surface of the whole earth, without touching the ground; and the goat had a notable horn between his eyes. Then he came to the ram that had two horns, which I had seen standing beside the river, and ran at him with furious power. And I saw him confronting the ram; he was moved with

rage against him, attacked the ram, and broke his two horns. There was no power in the ram to withstand him, but he cast him down to the ground and trampled him; and there was no one that could deliver the ram from his hand. Therefore the male goat grew very great; but when he became strong, the large horn was broken, and in place of it four notable ones came up toward the four winds of heaven. And out of one of them came a little horn which grew exceedingly great toward the south, toward the east, and toward the Glorious Land" (Daniel 8:3-9).

Gabriel then interpreted the dream to Daniel later in the chapter.

"The ram which you saw, having the two horns—they are the kings of Media and Persia. And the male goat is the kingdom of Greece. The large horn that is between its eyes is the first king. As for the broken horn and the four that stood up in its place, four kingdoms shall arise out of that nation, but not with its power. And in the latter time of their kingdom, When the transgressors have reached their fullness, A king shall arise, Having fierce features, Who understands sinister schemes. His power shall be mighty, but not by his own power; He shall destroy fearfully, And shall prosper and thrive; He shall destroy the mighty, and also the holy people. Through his cunning He shall cause deceit to prosper under his rule; And he shall exalt himself in his heart. He shall destroy many in their prosperity. He shall even rise against the Prince of princes; But he shall be broken without human means" (Daniel 8:20-25).

The nature of the animals used played an important role in the imagery of this vision.

Goats will easily revert from a domesticated state to a wild state. They are one of the domesticated animals that reverts the easiest into an untamed nature.

Shepherds can without difficulty separate their sheep from goats. They can train them to go one way or the other when separation of the herd is needed. This picture is what Jesus had in mind when he was describing the separating of the sheep from the goats in the first passage used in this chapter from Matthew. Look again at this passage with the addition of a couple of verses.

> "All the nations will be gathered before Him, and He will separate the one from another, as a shepherd divides his sheep from the goats. And He will set the sheep on His right hand, but the goats on the left. Then the King will say to those on His right hand, 'Come, you blessed of My Father, inherit the kingdom prepared for you from the foundation of the world.' ...Then he will also say to those on the left hand, 'Depart from Me, you cursed, into the everlasting fire prepared for the devil and his angels'" (Matthew 25:32-34, 41).

In this passage, Jesus used sheep and goats as analogies to just and wicked men. After looking at the nature of sheep in another chapter, and goats in this one, it stands to reason that Jesus used goats for the example of the wicked ones. Goats will always tend to go their own way and not follow the Shepherd Christ.

This is just one more example of how God used the inspired writers to include things He created in nature to teach us so we may gain a better understanding of His way.

Sources consulted:

Florida A & M University, Bulletin II. Vol. I, "Facts About Goats", by Angela McKenzie-Jakes, Extension Animal Science Specialist

Manners and Customs of Bible Lands, Fred K. Wight

Breeds of Livestock, Department of Animal Science, Oklahoma State University

World Land Trust

Macdonald, D. et al (2001). *The New Encyclopedic of Mammals.* Oxford University Press, UK

Wilson, D. & Mittermeier, R. eds (2011). *Handbook of the Mammals of the World, Vol 2.* Hoofed Mammals, Lunx Edicious, Barcelona

Orr, James, M.A.D.D. General Editor. "Entry for Sackcloth." *International Standard Bible Encyclopedia.* 1915

PAN: Greekgodsandgoddesses.net. Greek Gods and Goddesses. February 7, 2017

Greek Mythology. John Richard Thornhill Pollard, A.W.H. Adkins. July 18, 2019

About the Authors

Dr. Robert Bonner is a mixed-animal veterinarian and owner of Nashville Animal Hospital in Nashville, AR. He has been practicing veterinary medicine for fifteen years. Robert earned his Bachelor of Science from the University of Arkansas in 2001. He earned his Doctor of Veterinary Medicine (DVM) from Oklahoma State University College of Veterinary Medicine in 2005 and is a member of the American Association of Bovine Practitioners, the American Veterinary Medical Association, and the Arkansas Veterinary Medical Association. Robert does extensive work in bovine reproduction and herd health plan development as well as small animal medicine and orthopedics. Robert is an active leader in 4-H in the field of Veterinary Science, and he hosts monthly meetings for students at his veterinary hospital. He also frequently gives presentations about various aspects of beef cattle production at cooperative extension events and Cattlemen's meetings. Robert and his wife, Megan, and their two children, Morgan and Alex, live on a beef cattle farm, and the children exhibit Simmental cattle at livestock shows. Robert is a deacon at the Saratoga church of Christ in Saratoga, AR. He is a song leader, is very involved with Vacation Bible School, and is a teacher for the high school and adult classes.

John Allen lives in Lingleville, TX with his wife, Amy. They have 2 daughters and seven grandchildren. He is a graduate of Tarleton State University with a bachelor's degree in Animal Science. Before his retirement in 2010, he had a 29-year career with the Texas

AgriLife Extension as an agriculture agent in west Texas focusing on education and assistance to ranchers in the sheep and goat industry. John served on numerous local, regional and state task forces and committees related to the sheep, goat, range and wildlife industries, including being a member of the Texas Sheep and Goat Industry Improvement Task Force and member of the Texas Sheep and Goat Raiser's Association. He also served as a member of the Texas Total Resource Management (Agriculture) Advisory Steering Committee and helped teach ranch management schools for producers. He has been a part-time rancher for many years with sheep, cattle and goats. He is currently a licensed realtor specializing in farm and ranch property.

John is a recipient of the honored award of County Extension Agent-Texas Section of Society of Range Management, and the Outstanding County Extension Agent- Agriculture for Outstanding Contribution to the Sheep and Goat Industry-Texas Sheep and Goat Raiser's Association, and one of the Agent of the Year awards for the National and Texas County Agent Agriculture Associations.

John served as an elder of the Lord's church at the Northside congregation in Del Rio, TX. John and Amy are presently members of the Westside congregation in Stephenville where John serves as an elder.

William B. Baker, Jr. was educated at Texas A&M University (B.S. Wildlife & Fisheries Science 1977); University of Houston Clear Lake (M.S. Environmental Sciences 1986). He has worked as a Marine Biologist for Texas Parks & Wildlife Department for 6 years. Then, Environmental Manager for NRG Energy and its predecessor companies, 34 years.

Bill says: "For four decades I was blessed with the opportunity to work in the great outdoors in a profession I truly enjoyed. My job responsibilities varied over time, but my primary role was to evaluate ecological impacts of a variety of power generation facilities across the United States, including nuclear, natural gas, coal, wind, and solar. In many instances a key aspect of ecological impact evaluations included a variety of avian surveys. The advent of wind turbines and solar arrays brought a significant focus to avian interaction with these technologies, which subsequently significantly increased my participation in avian surveys in a variety of states. Additionally, my work involved management and implementation of a variety of habitat restoration projects across the United States, including forests, prairies, steams and riverbeds, intertidal marshes, offshore and inshore reefs, and freshwater marshes. Many of these projects received awards from a variety of organizations, including the Environmental Protection Agency, Texas General Land Office, Ecological Society of America, Edison Electric Institute, National Estuary Programs, U.S. Fish & Wildlife Service, and the Galveston Bay Foundation. I am currently retired from NRG Energy as Senior Manager of Ecology & Natural Resources. I have been a member of the church of Christ which meets in Bacliff, TX for over 40 years, and currently serve as an elder there."

Dr. Mark Bailey is a general dentist that resides in Fort Smith, AR, and serves as a shepherd for the Northside church of Christ, Greenwood, AR. Mark holds a B.S. in Zoology from the University of Arkansas, a Doctorate of Dental Surgery from Baylor College of Dentistry, is a fellow of the Pierre Fauchard Academy, the International College of Dentists, and the American College of Dentists. He has practiced in Waldron, AR, for 36 years, is both on staff and a Board Trustee for Mercy Hospital, Fort Smith, a Director for Delta Dental of Arkansas, a member of the ADA, and President of the RVDA.

Mark has been an avid hunter, fisherman, and conservationist since his youth; beginning his hunting career at 4 years of age following in his Dad's footsteps on small game hunts. Archery hunting for big game and turkey hunting are his favorite pursuits and he has hunted from Mississippi to Montana and virtually every state in between.

He has pursued big game since the mid 1960's and has considerable knowledge of the game species he pursues and couples that with a keen interest in habitat management for both game and non-game species alike, with an emphasis on deer and turkeys. Dr. Bailey has served on a special committee on Whitetail Deer management for the Arkansas Game and Fish Commission and as an officer for the Arkansas State Chapter of the NWTF.

Mark has been married to Janet Bailey for nearly 38 years, and they have two children, Marcus and Jordan, one son-in-law Clint Anglin, and two grandchildren, Reese Ann and Ford Marcus. Everyone in the family(except Janet) hunts and enjoys the outdoors. Perhaps his greatest love is serving the saints at Northside, and preaching and teaching God's word at home and in the region of western Arkansas.

Dr. Robert W Perkins, DVM, graduated from Texas A&M University in 1981 with degrees in Biomedical Science, Veterinary Science and a Doctorate of Veterinary Medicine. The first 30 years of his practice life were "mixed animal" which included small animals, farm animals and exotics.

Rob and his business partner started Tejas Veterinary Clinic in Corpus Christi, TX in 1998. He is serving his second term as President of the Coastal Bend Veterinary Medical Association.

He has been married to the former Julie Bedwell for 47 years from which union produced a son and daughter. They have been blessed with six grandchildren. In addition, they have owned a multitude of animals; cats, dogs, chickens, turkeys, geese, ducks, cattle and a beloved horse.

Rob has served as an Elder at Parkway Church of Christ for 23 years as of this writing.

In his spare time Rob writes a blog (religious articles) plays competitive volleyball, is a published genealogist and generally likes working outside at their home and ranch.

Dr. Ken Osborne earned the A.A. degree from Florida College in 1971, then went to Tennessee Technological University where he was awarded a double major in Animal Science and Biology, then the DVM from the University of Tennessee in 1985.

Dr. Osborne is married to Cindy Brown and they have two children, Daniel and Jennifer. He preached locally in Wichita Falls, TX, Corpus Christi, TX, and Cookeville, TN. He is currently a member of an elder for the Kleinwood church of Christ in Spring, TX.

His veterinary career includes Associate Veterinarian in Mineola, TX (1985-1986), Associaite Veterinarian in Spring, TX (1986-1993), then Head Veterinarian/Owner in Spring, TX (1993 to the present).

Dr. Osborne says, "Over my career I have primarily worked with dogs and cats but have also worked with horses, cattle, large cats, reptiles, birds, insectivores and various small mammal: "the Lord God made them all."

Dr. Stewart Coffman attended the California State Polytechnic University and the Universität Tübingen, in Tübingen, Germany, majoring in Microbiology. He attended Baylor College of Medicine in Houston, TX and graduated with his medical degree in 1991. After completing an internship in Internal Medicine at Baylor, he finished his residency in Emergency Medicine at UC San Diego. He received his MBA with a focus in Healthcare Management from UT Dallas.

Dr. Coffman is the EMS Medical Director for the Lewisville Fire Department. He has served as Medical Director and Tactical Physician for the FBI in Dallas/Fort Worth for 20 years. He is currently a Senior Vice President with Envision Physician Services in DFW.

For most of his early life he wanted to be a veterinarian and has always loved animals, especially dogs. An avid bird hunter, he has bred, raised and trained Labradors for many years. His favorite days afield are spent on a horse with a brace of upland dogs ranging across the prairie chasing elusive grouse.

From **Dr. Kevin Shurtleff**: "I was raised in the church. My parents and grandparents were all members of the church. My father worked for Prudential Insurance making agricultural loans and we moved about every five years. We moved to McAllen, TX when I was in the fourth grade and worshiped with the Laurel Heights Church of Christ. This great group of Christians would be the most influential congregation in my life, and the place where I would meet my future wife, Kay Garner. We moved to Seguin, TX when I was in the eighth grade, and met with the Pecan Valley congregation in San Antonio until my parents started a church in Seguin. After high school, I attended Texas A&M University where I worshiped with the Twin City congregation. I graduated from Texas A&M Veterinary School in 1986. As a senior veterinary student I received the Swine Medicine Proficiency Award. After veterinary school I took a job in Belton, TX working for another Christian, Harold Edwards, DVM. After one year in Belton, I moved to Mesquite, TX because I wanted to live in a big city and work with pet and exotic animals. I moved to Harlingen, TX in 1991 to get married, and again got to worship with the Laurel Heights congregation. After three years Kay and I moved back to Mesquite where we purchased Dallas County Veterinary Hospital and have lived ever since. We worship with the Campbell Road church of Christ in Garland, TX, and love this group also."

Made in the USA
Middletown, DE
18 March 2023